# In the Land of the Midnight Sun

## A Coming-of-Age Summer
## Far From Home – 1968

Third in the Series

## Look Out! Here Comes Summer
### My Incredible College Summers

*A Series of Books Describing the Summer*
*Life & Times of Charlie Ledbetter 1966–1970*

# Charles C. Ledbetter

Editor: Frances King, The Memoir Network
Cover & interior design: Sally Lunt, The Memoir Network
Photos: Charles C. Ledbetter & various credited sources

Books may be purchased for educational and promotional use.
Please contact the author at charlescledbetter.com.

ISBN: 978-1-7329339-6-5

# Dedication

To my life-long friend, John R. St. Clair, DDS, MS
in Orthodontics and Dentofacial Orthopedics, PA, and
veteran of the U.S. Army, who trusted me enough to climb
in his 1967 Pontiac and drive from Texas to Alaska
to spend the summer. His steady demeanor, frugal ways, and
winning personality—to say nothing of his fishing skills—
made the summer of 1968 unforgettable.

# Acknowledgements

Several people contributed to the completion of this book. I offer my thanks to all, including my wife, Sharon, and my good friend, the honorable James Patrick Vandello for their patience, guidance, and early reading of my drafts, and for John R. St. Clair for sharing with me his memories and photos from the summer of 1968.

The memory of Joe Nicewarner, a Cochran County pioneer, teacher, civic leader, and pillar of my home town, who took an interest in two young country boys from his community and graciously helped us explore the possibilities and then the reality of an Alaskan adventure.

Thanks also to Frances King, Sally Lunt, and Denis Ledoux of The Memoir Network for their professional guidance and assistance in bringing the stories of my incredible college summers to the printed page.

# Table of Contents

# Introduction

*"There are two things parents should give their children: roots and wings. Roots to give them bearing and a sense of belonging, but also wings to help free them from constraints and prejudices and give them other ways to travel (or rather, to fly)."*

Johann Wolfgang von Goethe

I never met anyone who did not respect my daddy. He spoke little, but when he spoke people listened. I remember a conversation between us from the summer of 1963. The ideas planted by that conversation changed my life, especially the summers of 1966 through 1970.

We were sitting on rough-hewn log benches in the lobby of the Old Faithful Lodge in Yellowstone National Park, waiting for the next expected eruption of the geyser. My mother and three of my sisters had left us to our own devices while they visited the gift shop. From experience, we knew several minutes, if not an hour, awaited us. We hoped their return would come before the predicted eruption of Old Faithful.

"Would you like a coke?" my daddy asked.

"Sure," I said.

He motioned to a young man wearing an Old Faithful Lodge golf shirt and khaki slacks. He came over directly and welcomed us to Yellowstone. Before we ordered anything, my daddy started asking questions. "Where are you from? Are you in college? Do you like your job? What's the best thing about being here?" I thought the fellow might show annoyance, but he appeared pleased that someone asked about *him*, and not just about the park.

We learned the waiter hailed from Terre Haute, Indiana, attended Purdue University as a sophomore, loved his job, and, other than the beautiful natural surroundings, he liked most being around the ladies his age. He said this summer job ranked at the top of all his jobs thus far. He took our order for coffee and a coke, carefully explaining that each would cost twenty-five cents. Although taken aback, my daddy did not object, although he knew that the price nearly equaled the price of a gallon of gasoline and was double the price of these same items in our hometown.

The waiter soon returned with our drinks: hot coffee in a mug and an ice-filled glass with Coca Cola. Daddy paid, leaving a dime for a tip, but kept talking. "How did you get this job? How much do they pay? How did you travel here? When did you report and when do you go home? Are you traveling elsewhere this summer? What do your parents do in Terre Haute? Where is Terre Haute anyway?"

Given the friendliness of the waiter, we learned that he had seen an ad at Purdue and applied for jobs at Yellowstone, Glacier, and Grand Canyon National Parks; he received $25 per week plus room and board; he drove a 1958 Ford Fairlane from Indiana; he had arrived June first and would stay until September fourth; he planned to see the Tetons, Devil's Tower, and the Badlands National Monument on his journey home; his father ran the water/sewer department for the city; his mother taught school; and Terre Haute lay along the Wabash River and Interstate 70 on the western edge of Indiana.

In return for all that information, my daddy said: "Thanks for the drinks. I hope you enjoy the rest of your summer and the trip home."

I felt somewhat worldly, but had never heard of Terre Haute, Indiana. My travels had included Ruidoso, New Mexico; Corpus Christi, Texas; and three days in Dallas while Daddy attended the Texas Bar convention. All those trips included my family, but I did travel without family to Colorado Springs, for the 50th Anniversary Boy Scouts of America Jamboree in 1960.

The trip to Yellowstone marked a high-water mark for family vacations. We could not afford fancy or long-term trips. By 1963 my two older sisters had married and missed that family trip. My hunch was that Daddy wanted a big vacation before another sister married or left for college, so we took off. We made several stops in several western states before Yellowstone. We would see several more before getting home. No other vacation before had included as many stops and nowhere near as many miles. As it turned out, none of our other vacations changed my future the way this one did.

"What did you think about that fellow and his job?" my daddy asked without emphasis.

"Sounded like fun to me," I replied.

My daddy went on to say he had felt burdened by responsibilities since age fifteen when he had left home to go live with an uncle. During the 1930s his family lost crops in consecutive years and struggled to feed themselves—himself and five siblings. At age fifteen, he worked in a drugstore and slept in a backroom with a shotgun. His experience had not included vacations and travel.

11

"I wanted to travel some, but it never worked out," he said casually, though not directly to me. "Later, I was in school, working, trying to get by, and never had time or money for travels. Then when Mother and I married, we needed every dollar to support you kids."

I felt that this reminiscing was meant to tell me something, but I remained quiet.

"Maybe you could get a job like this when you are in college," he suggested.

I noted that he did not use "if" in the sentence. Me going to college was already settled as an expectation, not an aspiration. Maybe the summers between college years could provide opportunities.

Finally, I told him I had "never thought about it before."

After that day, I thought about it many times.

Soon my mother and sisters returned from the gift shop, and we set off to see the great geyser, Old Faithful.

Tales of what I did during my summer vacations constitute this series of four books. I worked as a congressional intern in Washington D.C.; served as the horse wrangler at an exclusive all-girls summer camp in the Colorado Rockies; joined a high school friend to drive a 1967 Pontiac to Alaska and stay three months; and, after graduating college, began law school, received an induction notice from Uncle Sam, and entered the U.S. Marine Corps.

I remain blessed that my parents had vision, loved me, supported my dreams, and encouraged me. Those blessings led to people, places, and experiences that at age sixteen never seemed possible to me.

This introduction concludes with a quote from one of my favorite authors. Kurt Vonnegut opens *Slaughterhouse Five* with

12

this sentence: "All of this happened, more or less." The same is true of these adventures. I hope you enjoy these stories.

# In the Land of the Midnight Sun

# Chapter 1
# Change of Plans

For years I wanted to work in the outdoors, preferably in a National Park or with the Forest Service somewhere in the western states. Alaska because of its remoteness, wilderness, and strange allure, topped my list of desired places for summer work. However, despite my best efforts and several formal and informal contacts, the summer of 1968 would not include such jobs. This unfortunate circumstance led to a change in my plans.

For the two previous years I attempted to make arrangements with the Forest Service for summer work in Alaska. Congressman George Mahon gave me a recommendation and contacted top officials in the U.S. Department of Agriculture, including the Chief of the Forest Service. The congressman also sent a letter of recommendation to the Bureau of Land Management in Anchorage supporting my search for a summer job in Alaska.

Alaska, because of its location far away from the forty-eight contiguous states, had prerequisites attached to many of its seasonal jobs, especially with the governmental agencies. One required all workers to present themselves on location without governmental aid or reimbursement. This obviously created a big advantage for local residents and students. Even if a student from the lower forty-eight could comply, he took second priority to locals.

A different opportunity for summer employment came from plans for building the trans-Alaskan pipeline reaching from the far north of the state to the port of Valdez on the Gulf of Alaska. Oil discovery in Prudhoe Bay on the Arctic Ocean in 1968 created a need for transporting oil eight hundred miles to the ice-free, deep-water port of Valdez. The ambitious plan to design, construct, operate, and maintain the pipeline required thousands of workers and would extend over a decade. As with many government-private projects the plan developed slowly, and the summer of 1968 came too soon for most of the related jobs.

I had one other longshot for a summer job in Alaska. The former Superintendent of Schools and current County Treasurer in my hometown heard from my dad about my dream of going to Alaska. It turned out his sister married a man who recently retired from the Government Accounting Office and lived in Anchorage, Alaska. This family friend promised to relay my idea of working in Alaska to his sister and brother-in-law to see if they could provide any suggestions. While the early communications along this path encouraged me, nothing concrete appeared during the spring months, and I needed to get on with my plans.

In addition to my interest in mountains, forests, rivers and the lure of the West, my parents told a story of their early dream/plan/aspiration to move to Alaska soon after they married and raise a family. The plan, whimsical at best, involved having twin boys to supply some of the needed labor to establish a life on the frontier. This story of their plans struck a note with my imagination and, since it never came to fruition, maybe I could experience some of the things of their dreams. Because I lived in a temperate climate, I could not imagine a winter of sub-zero temperatures. The family story and the mild summer weather made the summer job attractive to me, but perhaps another year.

# Heading to Nashville

Instead of pursuing another job in the wilderness I defaulted to the pursuit of filthy lucre. One of my friends at Baylor University worked two earlier summers at the Southwestern Company, a Bible and educational book publisher based in Nashville, Tennessee. He told the story of a successful summer selling Bibles and books door-to-door and making a ton of money. Five thousand dollars for a summer's work sounded outrageous to me, but it caught my interest. I worked the entire previous summer at Camp Shoshoni for $550 plus room and board. Making five thousand dollars over the summer would soothe any disappointment from missing an adventure. Besides, selling books door-to-door sounded like an adventure, just of another sort. The potential to make that kind of money pulled me in and my friend convinced me I would be good at it.

The job included some drawbacks. It required a week's training in Nashville and then an assignment to a location not revealed until the end of the training. Most of the jobs landed in the southeastern United States, but no one got a guarantee of a particular place. I needed to provide my own transportation and living expenses over the summer, and this created quite an unknown for planning. My friend said I could get an advance against sales, but needed to send paperwork proving those sales before the company sent any advance. As a practical matter no advance would arrive until mid-July. That left me with six weeks of expenses before any aid arrived.

Feeling confident in my own ability to talk the talk and learn the sales pitches, I signed up. Hearing my friend tell of filling a suitcase with over $4,000; his commission at summer's end minus advances, all in single dollar bills to impress his parents, pushed away any indecision on my part. Several acquaintances at Baylor worked these summer jobs and confirmed the opportunity. I was set to go.

At the end of classes the third week of May, I began my travels to attend the training sessions in Nashville on June 2, taking a circuitous route to the Music City. I drove home from college to see my family and load up needed clothes for the summer. I stayed two days, a length my mother disapproved of because of its brevity, but not one to criticize her only son, she made no objection to me. However, my oldest sister gave me an earful about my self-centered plans and recommended that I stay longer. But I had a girlfriend in Denver, Hungie Hunter, and that romance grew more serious by the month. I wanted to see her before I took off for the summer to parts unknown as a Bible salesman, so I included Denver on my not so direct travels to Nashville.

While driving the five hundred plus miles to Denver from Morton, Texas it never occurred to me I would repeat the drive before a fortnight passed. The weather was hot and dry, and my Volkswagen bug, nicknamed the Chuck Wagon, chugged along the highways never exceeding sixty-five miles per hour. On the ascent of Raton Pass at the New Mexico-Colorado border the car proved capable of only 45 mph with the gas pedal pushed full throttle. The pace gave me time to enjoy the scenery, but also made me impatient to cover the distance in less time.

After a few days in Denver, the VW and I headed east to St. Louis to see my future in-laws. That 850 miles distance took a day and a half with me sleeping in rest stops along the way. I remember the not-quite-ready for harvest wheat fields stretching as far as the eye could see across Kansas. The excitement of getting to my training and new job kept me enthused. The idea of earning lots of money in the coming months pushed my car-riding tolerance as I continued the journey at the VW's slow, but steady, pace across the heartland of America.

I rested a bit in St. Louis and enjoyed a steak dinner on the grill courtesy of my girlfriend's parents. As I recall the only hiccup came when in response to how I wanted my steak I responded I wanted it well done. Mr. Hunter, who headed a large meat processing operation across the Mississippi River in East St. Louis, Illinois, remarked, "Not at my house, you don't," and informed me my steak would be medium. It came a tad on the rare side of medium and opened my taste buds to new adventures in steak grilling. To this day, thanks to Mr. Hunter, I prefer my steaks medium rare.

I left St. Louis on Saturday, June 1st and headed to Anna, Illinois to visit Hungie's maternal grandmother. Anna, with its adjoining town of Jonesboro, marked its claim to fame as one of the sites for the Lincoln-Douglas debates more than a century earlier. Granny Robinson, as everyone called her, was a delightful lady who said exactly what she thought and showed a dry sense of humor. We met during the Christmas holidays of 1967, and I looked forward to stopping by for a visit. She generously supplied a stopover on my way southeast to Nashville.

When I arrived mid-afternoon on Saturday, Granny Robinson welcomed me with a pitcher of iced tea and chocolate chip cookies. The radio in her kitchen carried the broadcast of the St. Louis Cardinals baseball game and while Granny appeared to focus on me during our conversation, she also kept track of the game's status and often interjected a running commentary on what the Cards should do as strategy for the coming innings. She told me Bob Gibson, the fire-balling pitcher for the Cardinals, would set records that summer, and he did. She also casually mentioned he was a skillful player, despite being Black.

Southern Illinois kept some of the antipathy for black people I experienced in Texas.

## The Southwestern Company

On Sunday I headed out across the wooded, hilly country-side of southern Illinois and northwestern Kentucky on the way to Nashville. The training for the Southwestern Company began with a BBQ dinner and reception at 6 p.m. Crossing rivers with substantial water flows and names I never heard amazed me although I had traveled some of the area before on the way to the National Boy Scout Jamboree in Valley Forge, Pennsylvania, four summers before in 1964. Coming from such an arid part of the country, a county with no running water, made flowing rivers a continued treat for my unaccustomed eyes. I drove the VW across a huge bridge across the Ohio River and into Paducah, Kentucky. The copious water flow under the bridge boggled my mind.

I arrived with a couple of hours to spare and got situated in a dormitory next to the training site. Everyone received a packet of samples, sales pitches, and price sheets along with the admonition we needed to memorize them as quickly as possible. The training would require us to present sales pitches to our group of eight to ten folks. The staff also greeted me with enthusiasm and told me of the great adventure lying ahead.

The dinner was outside in the hot, humid air of middle Tennessee. The affair included no alcohol servings, but plenty of sweet tea and water. Most of us took advantage of the drinks and tried to stay hydrated while we waited for the introductory remarks.

Soon "Chief" Wilson, the sales manager for Southwestern stepped to the microphone and started his remarks. The Chief part to his name reputedly came from his Cherokee Scots Irish heritage and he looked the part. Tall, thin, with dark hair and high cheekbones, Chief held everyone's attention and welcomed us to the Southwestern family. His talk reminded me of a cross between a Zig Ziglar motivational speech and a tent revival sermon as he mixed in personal responsibility, family ties, our God-given talents, generosity toward others, and a sense of self-determination.

I recall Chief telling a joke making fun of door-to-door Bible salesmen. One of the best salesmen from the prior year spoke with a pronounced stutter. While many thought this impediment might dampen his effectiveness, his sales consistently ranked among the top sales company wide. The Chief called the fellow in and asked the secret to his success and the salesman replied he worked hard each day and kept going to the next door after someone told him no. Chief pushed him, saying there must be more to his success because most of the other top salespeople did those same things. Finally, the fellow said, "I, I, I ju-ju-just, tel-tel-tell, whoever answers the door, wou-wou-would they like to buy this Bible, or do they wa-wa-want me to re-re-read it to them? The crowd roared and the Chief said he now understood the secret to this salesman's success.

The next morning the training started in earnest. We got assignments into groups of eight to ten people. My group had no women although the training class included about ten women out of 185 trainees. Right off the bat, the leader asked for a volunteer to deliver one of the sales pitches included in our packet of information. I did not volunteer although I had read the materials the night before. The fellow's pitch went on for about two minutes before the leader called a halt. Next, he asked the group to give evaluations of what the man did right and what he could improve. I lauded the fellow for his bravery in going first. Others mentioned he obviously needed to polish the pitch because he

21

struggled to move from one point to the next. The leader showed emotional and professional support by congratulating the presenter on his voice, tone, and diction and echoed the group in saying the speaker needed more practice.

The first couple of hours went quickly as half of the group got to make a presentation before facing the group evaluations. I felt a bit tongue-tied during my pitch, but felt it went okay, not great. The evaluations followed the pattern of the earlier presenters. Before taking a break at 10:30 a.m. the leader started a talk designed to encourage competition and dedication. He declared two to three of us would not make one month in the field, only those dedicated and willing to put in the effort would survive and become successful. I had heard similar pitches from football and basketball coaches on the first day of practice in high school and college and took the talk in stride. I felt comfortable with learning the pitches and background information and knew my experience giving tours of the Capitol in Washington D.C. would kick in and allow me to smoothly present the material. The part I did not feel comfortable about came from the uncertainty of my assigned location for the summer. What if they sent me to some Podunk, low-income area where people had little enthusiasm for buying Bibles? At the break I mentioned this to our group leader.

He came prepared for the question. He launched into a slick, pat response. It did not convey any sincerity, at least to me. Several of our team eagerly awaited his answer because it weighed on everyone. His glib answer included variations of "we've always done it this way," to "you will understand later." Neither appeared to assuage the anxiety of the group.

After lunch, the Chief gave the entire group another pep talk emphasizing the money made by the top salespeople from previous years. He intimated outrageous numbers such as $5,000,

$7,000, and $10,000 were possible if we learned all the pitches by heart and worked in a disciplined manner all summer, refusing to take days off other than Sundays. He cautioned us against breaking discipline, claiming that bad habit was the main source of failure by the sales force. He touched on the location issue by telling us the company screened all locations for population, per capita income, churches per 10,000 citizens, and families with children. Selections included no unsuitable areas. The insinuation was any failures would result from our individual failures, not the company's selection process. He concluded his talk by saying he would pray for the success of each and every one of us.

The training sessions continued through the afternoon and after the dinner meal. We concluded about 9 p.m. when most of us eagerly sought a shower and some down time. Of course, the team leaders encouraged individual study or pairing off with another in our dorm to practice our sales pitches. Some of the fellows followed along the company line, but I deferred by saying I needed to study on my own more than I needed practice giving the sales pitch. After reading the materials, I hit my bunk around 10 p.m. and slept well. I looked forward to getting through the week and starting to make some money.

Tuesday and Wednesday followed a similar pattern. Our group practiced presentations and offered evaluations. I noticed the evaluations, especially from the team leader, took on a harder edge compared to those offered the day before. Once the team heard this from the leader, the individual critiques also became harsher as if each one wanted to add a punishing element to their evaluations. Too slow, too long, too wordy, did not stay on topic, wandered around with your talk; these became the pattern instead of encouragement and acknowledging progress. I recall not feeling good about the second day's activities but not mentioning anything to others or especially, our team leader.

On Wednesday we heard the news of an attempted assassination of presidential candidate Robert F. Kennedy at a hotel in Los Angeles. The full schedule of classes and practice presentations prevented any updates but several of us talked about it and expressed shock at the news. Coming within two months of Martin Luther King, Jr.'s assassination and the domestic riots and protests that followed, these developments caused many of us to wonder what could possibly come next.

# A Phone Call

The afternoon session dragged a bit and I looked forward to the dinner break at 6 p.m., expecting to hear more news about Kennedy. The pattern from the first two days allowed an hour for the meal and leisure time before hitting the practice sessions again from 7 to 9 p.m. I munched on a cheeseburger and some fries when I heard someone call my name.

"Is Ledbetter in here?"

I raised my hand wondering what brought up my name. "Here."

"You have a call," came the response followed by a wave toward the hallway outside the dining hall.

The man calling my name directed me toward a pay phone at the end of the hallway. I wondered who on earth called me. I only gave the contact number to my parents and my girlfriend with strict instructions not to call unless something important merited it. I promised to call at the end of the week and tell them the location I received for the summer, but the training would take all of my time during the week. With those names in mind I drew a blank when the fellow holding the phone handed it to me and said, "It's some guy named John."

I offered a puzzled, "Hello?"

I quickly learned the John on the other end of the line was John St. Clair, one of my best friends from our hometown. Although a couple of years younger than me, John and I enjoyed a long-standing friendship through Little League Baseball, Boy Scouts, high school sports, and close family ties. Our fathers, mothers and siblings had been friends most of our lives and we knew each other well. Because I recalled John's father passed away while I worked in Washington D.C., my first thought included someone dying, being in an accident, or some other unexpected event and brought a quick drop to my stomach, but John quickly assured me everything was fine. He had other news.

"Mr. Nicewarner's brother-in-law called your dad today and said he could get us some jobs if we got to Anchorage in the next week to ten days. Do you still want to go?"

John and I had discussed a trip to Alaska for several months but gave up that dream when things did not pan out.

"What?" My dumbstruck reply barely passed my lips before John excitedly told me of the call from our contact in Alaska, the possibility of jobs, his mother's permission if we wanted to go, my dad giving him my contact phone number at the Southwestern Company, how we needed to decide quickly, he understood if I wanted to pass, but if I wanted to go, we could drive his 1967 Pontiac. He added he would pass on the opportunity if I could not make it, but wanted me to have the opportunity to think it over.

"Wow," I muttered as I tried to collect my thoughts to respond. John reminded me of our dream to take on such an endeavor and having someone local to get us jobs made it all possible. He did not need to remind me this might be our only chance for such an adventure.

Without really thinking too much about the planning, I almost shouted into the phone, "Let's do it!"

I told John I needed a couple of days to get home and we could talk more over that time, but he should begin preparations and I would assemble my clothes, money, etc., when I got home. We tentatively made a plan to leave on Saturday, June 8, just three days away. That allowed two days of travel, a day to get ready and visit with my family, and then a departure. Despite the frantic schedule and miles of travel in a slow-moving VW, the prospect of being in Alaska for the summer, thrilled me.

With a huge grin I returned to the dining hall and my colleagues finishing their meal. I announced in a voice loud enough to reach every one of the 150 or so people in the room, "I'm going to Alaska!"

# Chapter 2
# Mr. Ledbetter

My sudden decision raised several questions. How do I resign from the Southwestern Company? Would they protest? When could I start for Texas? Was the VW up for another 1,000 miles? Did I know what I had done?

Thus far I made no commitments to Southwestern other than my presence at the training session and commitment to working the summer. I signed no formal contract. Those formalities came with the designation of a work location for the summer, expected on Saturday morning. All summer workers received the designation of independent contractors, not employees of the company so I expected no difficulties in severing ties and going my way. Despite no formal ties, I felt an obligation to tell the company why I changed my mind. I did not feel comfortable getting in my car and driving away without an explanation.

I started with my team leader. He looked confused and answered the company never assigned anyone to Alaska. That confused me until I realized he thought I wanted the company to send me there. After explaining I needed to quit and not finish the training because I was going to Alaska, he caught on and said I could not quit without talking to Chief and the Chief already left for the day. I requested a meeting for first thing Thursday morning.

My dorm mates gathered around me and started asking lots of questions. Most wanted to know how I could leave this opportunity and head off for the 49th State without discussing it with anyone. Others expressed support and made comments much like the tried and true; "You only go around once." One person indicated he dreamed of going to Alaska and wondered if I needed another companion. I declined his offer.

I skipped the training session after dinner and gathered my clothes and shaving kit. Packing went easily because I brought few belongings with me to Tennessee. Next, I mentally checked off a route for driving home and estimated the time needed. West to Memphis, across Arkansas to Texarkana, then west toward Lubbock, I should be able to easily cover the thousand miles in two hard days of driving. After all, I spent two good days the week before driving 850 miles across Kansas and Missouri to St. Louis. Another 150 miles at this point seemed a cipher.

## A Relative in Tennessee

For some reason, as I plotted a drive west along Interstate 40 toward Memphis, a memory of a relative living near Milan, Tennessee popped into my mind. All I knew about Milan was it lay somewhere west of the Tennessee River, near Jackson, between Nashville and Memphis. I found Jackson along the Interstate on my map and searched for Milan. I found it about forty miles north of Jackson and plotted a plan to make a detour to see if I could find James Coleman Ledbetter.

Mr. Ledbetter was my great-grandfather's nephew. I had to look it up, but that means he and I are first cousins twice removed. At any rate he and his wife Nell lived in Milan in 1947 when my mother and daddy drove there to visit. My great-grandfather lived there also. I remember my mother, who was twenty-

28

nine years old, saying the small house had three, what seemed to her as elderly people: James, Nell and my great-grandfather, Henry Coleman Ledbetter. She remembered they had barely enough food for two people, much less three. At the time Henry was eighty-three and James and Nell probably in their fifties, twenty years or so older than my daddy. After a brief discussion, my parents loaded Henry in the car and brought him to Morton, Texas. I was a year old when he came and he lived with us another six years, dying at the age of eighty-nine. Mother recalled him rocking a cradle with his cane while he sat in an easy chair. I occupied the cradle.

Even though I remembered this story fairly well, I still faced a big problem. I had no address, no telephone number, no idea how to find the Ledbetter home in Milan, Tennessee. I wracked my brain for other memories and remembered there was a Post Office named Ledbetter, Tennessee near Milan and the home/small store was near the Ledbetter Gate to the Army Ammunition Depot. If I got close, surely, I could find someone to direct me to Mr. Ledbetter.

I awoke around 6 a.m. and bided my time waiting to meet with the Chief and bid adieu to the Southwestern Company. The humid air outside the dorm lacked the heat sure to arrive later in the day and felt good on my skin as I loaded everything into the Chuck Wagon. Breakfast went smoothly with only a couple of colleagues asking when I planned to leave and wishing me well. I could see others talking and pointing my direction leaving no doubt in my mind I was the topic of discussion that morning.

Around a quarter to nine the Chief arrived and made the rounds talking to the team leaders. When my leader's turn arrived, I stood in the background a few feet away. The Chief looked over the leader's shoulder at me and then resumed the conversation. Soon, however, Chief motioned for me to join him in the hallway.

"Are you crazy?" the Chief opened with a not so endearing line that carried his disapproval of my plan.

"No sir. This chance just happened, and it's been a dream of mine for some time. I feel I must take advantage of it. I don't know if I will ever get another chance."

"Well, you are passing up a terrific opportunity. Your leader told me you have enormous potential and I hate to see you walk away from it. Is your mind made up?"

Chief gave me a chance to change my mind, but did not press it any further. He concluded with, "Good luck on your travels."

By 9 a.m. I headed for Interstate 40 West. The assassination of Robert F. Kennedy dominated the news. A news bulletin came every few minutes with further details or supposition about the event. The initial reports included only brief details about emergency surgery on the presidential candidate, but the report of his death soon followed. Two hours later, just north of Jackson, I reached the cutoff for Milan and turned north. The sun was high, and the heat continued to climb as I neared Milan. I wondered how I might find Mr. Ledbetter.

I slowed down and began looking for a courthouse or official looking building where I might talk to someone. A radio station appeared on my left and I pulled into the parking lot thinking someone there should know the community and help me. I knew my hometown radio station dealt with all kinds of community news ranging from boll weevil infestations to weather, to local church news, and scheduled events in and around the town. Certainly, someone there knew about Ledbetter, Tennessee. My mind raced as I got out of the car and walked in.

A receptionist greeted me and expressed dismay at not understanding what I wanted, but she did hit the intercom for the station manager to see if he could help. A balding, fortyish fellow appeared and motioned me into his cubicle-office. He wore a short-sleeved shirt, a tie much wider than the current fashion, and no jacket. I repeated my quest for Mr. Ledbetter and Ledbetter, Tennessee. I remembered the Milan Army Ammunition plant had a Ledbetter gate into its sprawling grounds and added this detail to my story. The station manager said he knew nothing of Mr. Ledbetter, or a town called Ledbetter, but the Ledbetter gate to the plant was about a mile and a half northeast on Highway 79. He offered that someone out there, or the guard at the gate, would know more. With his directions I headed out Highway 79.

## James Coleman Ledbetter

Before I traveled two miles, I saw a white, clapboard house on the right with a sign; James C. Ledbetter Co., above the entrance. It was noon when I pulled into a driveway leading to the house. With sweat dripping from my nose, I hopped out and went to the door. I saw a screen door to the left of the sign and found it the only barrier to the inside. I looked into the house but could not see anyone. I knocked on the screen door. No answer. I knocked louder and longer. Still, no sound from inside.

After about a minute, with a full-throated call, I yelled: "Mr. Ledbetter?"

From inside the shadows a voice answered, "Yes."

"I am Charles Coleman Ledbetter," I answered again with a full voice.

"Come on in," the voice replied. I still did not see the source of the voice, but soon a tall, thin, grey-haired man appeared and pushed the screen door open.

He asked if I said, "*Charles Coleman Ledbetter.*" I nodded and confirmed my name. He stood about my height, six-foot one inch, and wore black work shoes, grey trousers, a long-sleeved grey shirt buttoned at the collar, with tan suspenders snapped, not buttoned, to his trousers which rode three inches or so above his waist. His white hair had receded toward the top of his head revealing a pale, broad forehead and his face bore long, bushy eyebrows and a large nose.

His grey-green eyes sparkled as he looked me over.

"I think we are kin." I offered.

"You must be M.C.'s boy." His mind and memory quickly recalled my daddy even though twenty years or more passed since they last saw each other. He turned and pointed toward a couch and easy chair in the front room. As I sat on the couch I glanced around quickly and noted a large radio on a stand, but no television.

He offered to fix me a sandwich, but I declined. From the looks of his small kitchen in the

James Coleman Ledbetter,
Milan, TN, June 1968

32

back I feared he had little to share with me and figured I could grab a hamburger once I got back on the road. We shared some iced tea and continued our visit. He asked what brought me to Gibson County, Tennessee, about my parents' health, my destination, how long could I stay, and how I found him. I quickly told him my story, about the job with the Southwestern Company and then the chance to spend the summer in Alaska. He asked me if I knew how far it was to Alaska?

We talked about my schooling at Baylor University and how I planned to attend law school. He recalled my daddy being a judge and commented on how he liked some lawyers. He left his comments about lawyers at that. He told me about running a small printing business making address labels and business cards and confirmed he no longer farmed any land. His large, gnarled hands showed at one time they endured many hours of manual labor beyond running a small print shop. I enjoyed the visit, the shade of the house, although it lacked air-conditioning, and the sweet tea. We talked without hesitation or a lack of questions and topics for over an hour. He seemed genuinely pleased I stopped by to see him.

He regaled me with stories of my great-grandfather. I learned he pursued various jobs and occupations throughout his lifetime without marked success and to his nephew at least, he was a bit of a dreamer. He mentioned Henry Coleman always dreamed of bigger and better endeavors and lived several places: Tennessee, Missouri, Arkansas, Texas, and California. He recalled how my parents came to visit and asked Henry Coleman to return with them to Texas. At first, according to Mr. Ledbetter, my great-grandfather expressed fear and anxiety about moving to Texas, but later wrote him of how much he enjoyed living with our family. Hearing these stories and receiving such a warm welcome, gave me a hoped-for connection and fondness for Mr. Ledbetter. Our meeting exceeded my expectations.

Unfortunately, my travel time ticked away each minute I sat in Mr. Ledbetter's front room, but I wanted to raise one question to him before I left.

I noted he, I, my daddy, and my great grandfather all shared a common middle name: Coleman. I wondered aloud about that recurring pattern among the males in our family. Mr. Ledbetter said he knew very well how the family came to use Coleman as a middle name for many.

Mr. Ledbetter sat back, crossed one leg over the other, and looked directly at me before speaking.

"Years ago, soon after the civil war, one of our ancestors married a woman with the maiden name of Coleman," he started the story. He continued that she came from east of the river and by then I understood he meant the Tennessee River, not the Mississippi River. Her folks farmed and raised some animals, much like the Ledbetter clan she married into, and she understood the ways of country, farm folks.

He described her as tall, slim, having hazel-green eyes and deep brown hair with a hint of auburn running through it. He mentioned she possessed fair looks, but the thing people loved more about her than her looks, was her kind and generous nature. She worked as hard as the men, cooked, cleaned for the family, nursed many when they came down sick, and always expressed a good-natured humor about herself. She was self-confident and as Mr. Ledbetter put it, not stuck on herself.

He recalled her apple pies as the best in the county and that she often became the first one to visit neighbors when someone took ill. She prayed for everyone, held up her end of the Baptist church, and became known in those parts as a fine, Christian woman.

Everyone genuinely loved her and counted on her for so many things and this family affection for her led one of our ancestors, he could not remember exactly who, to use her maiden name as the middle name for a son. He thought this was a generation or so before my great grandfather's and the practice became a tradition. Hence, Henry Coleman, Middleton Coleman, and Charles Coleman: great grandfather, father, and me. He could not explain how my grandfather became Irving Lytle Ledbetter and skipped the Coleman name, except to say he felt Henry Coleman expected to have another son who would bear the Coleman name, and it never happened. He mentioned how his father loved and admired this woman and how he wanted his son to bear the name. That was how he became James Coleman Ledbetter.

Feeling satisfied with hearing this family lore and taking over an hour of his time, I shifted my body on the couch thinking I should rise and say my goodbyes, but Mr. Ledbetter remained sitting erect and made no effort to move. He had more on his mind. His brow furrowed, his bushy eyebrows narrowed a bit, his jaw tightened, and he looked directly at me as if to offer some parting benediction. Then he said with a bitterness absent from all the preceding accolades and as if he needed to first spit on the ground, "But her folks wuz REPUBLICANS!"

His last remark surprised and tickled me.

Our short visit concluded, I asked if I could take his photo and promised to write. He wished me safe travels, vigorously shook my hand, and slapped me on the back as I turned toward my car.

"Give my best to your folks, and Alaska," his last words.

Soon I rejoined Interstate 40 and headed for Memphis basking in the good feelings produced by my visit with family. Alaska seemed a million miles away.

# In the Land of the Midnight Sun

## Chapter 3
# Getting Home and Ready to Go

Catching Interstate 40 just outside Jackson, Tennessee proved easy. My detour to Milan and Mr. Ledbetter's home took a little over two hours. The summer heat and humidity bore down on me and the car as I began calibrating time and distance to Texarkana, Texas. Once on Texas soil, I felt I could stop for a rest and get some sleep, but at this point the visit buoyed my spirits and I stood ready for a several hour drive toward home.

Seeking a Memphis radio station, expecting some blues, country, or hillbilly music—the music made famous in that town, I found only news reports. Visiting with a relative I never met, and hearing family stories caused me to completely forget the events of the day, week, and year. In many ways the respite buried all my worries, anxiety, and fears. The news jolted me back into the present.

# Events of Early 1968

Earlier that spring, on March 31, while driving back to Baylor after spending Easter vacation in Morton, I listened as President Lyndon Johnson made a radio address to the nation. I recall driving south of Comanche, Texas on Sunday evening on my way to Waco when the president's voice came on the radio.

I, and most of the world, expected an update on the Vietnam war and him urging support for his policies. The anti-war faction in the U.S. received a boost earlier that month when Eugene McCarthy received a surprisingly strong showing in the New Hampshire primary for the Democratic Party's nomination for president. Four days after that, Robert F. Kennedy announced his bid for the presidency. Many knew of the distaste Robert Kennedy had for President Johnson, but Kennedy's announcement took most people by surprise, including the president.

Near the end of the president's radio speech, he announced to the world, he *"would not seek, nor would he accept, the nomination of his party for another term as our president."* I almost ran off the road. Most people knew how Johnson loved the power of the presidency and could not fathom him walking away. His speech made it abundantly clear that was exactly what he intended to do.

Then, four days later came the assassination of Martin Luther King, Jr. in Memphis, Tennessee, the town I was approaching. My mind raced back to the evening I heard that news.

I functioned as the Resident Advisor (RA) for the second floor of Martin Hall at Baylor University, an all-male dormitory. The RA's job involved keeping the racket below three hundred decibels after 6 pm, making sure no one taped a Playboy Centerfold to the closet door, and trying to keep mayhem at acceptable levels. Martin Hall housed most of the athletes, so the constituency tended toward mesomorphs. Several outweighed me by one hundred pounds.

Some residents could match wits with anyone on campus, but others were a long way from being the sharpest knives in the drawer. 'Dumb jock' fit some perfectly. A few were serious about religion and academics, others just about sports. Most RAs were easy going, not wanting to be a hard ass to others on the floor, maybe because if someone's ass was going to get kicked, the RA became the candidate to receive it. We did this job in exchange for a credit toward our tuition. Baylor allowed this as payment, I thought to simplify the arrangement instead of paying us and then have us pay them back. This made a simple accounting procedure. We reported once a month to an adult supervisor, but operated on our own. I got along well with my floor mates and avoided hassles.

Baylor was the largest Southern Baptist (the conservative kind) Christian university in the world. Its spiritual heritage was unambiguously, even a little in your face, Christian. Most students and many professors believed in the literal interpretation of scriptures and the inerrancy of "The Word." When crossing the campus on foot one often met complete strangers stopping to ask if you accepted Jesus as your personal Lord and Savior? Baylor required mandatory attendance at Chapel for worship and Christian teachings Mondays and Wednesdays. Many professors added Christian commentary to their lectures—even if the link to geology/history/philosophy was tangential at best.

Academic excellence was another foundational principle for Baylor. It sought a mixture of interdisciplinary research with an international reputation for educational excellence and a faculty commitment to teaching and scholarship. Founded in 1845 Baylor, through the efforts of Baptist pioneers, was the oldest continually operating university in Texas. This combination of academics with a Christian flavor attracted me. Mostly, I remembered the tales my daddy and "double-uncle" Neal Rose told about their days at Baylor and sought that experience.

In step with the civil rights movement in the U.S. Baylor took steps to integrate its sports teams. Until the 1960's only white athletes played in the Southwest Conference. This changed on September 10, 1966, when John Westbrook, a black player for Baylor, took the field against Syracuse University. Westbrook, as we called him, lived in the Martin Hall. He was smart, articulate and could run like the wind.

On Thursday night, April 4, 1968, I sat at my desktop in my dorm room after supper time, maybe 6:30 pm, reading a world history lesson from class the day before. On most nights, the noise levels in the dorm stayed low until about 9 pm when most guys returned and started their stereos or horseplay with roommates. I wanted to finish my reading before the nightly ruckus started. Some nights I told folks to hold it down. This usually came later, between 9 and 10 p.m., that's when things got noisy. Most noise warnings came after 10 p.m.

Some more religiously inclined held a nightly prayer meeting at 10 p.m. in the third-floor lounge. That helped quiet down the entire dorm. The prayer meeting usually gathered 20 to 30 of the ninety-six residents. As a son, grandson, and great grandson of Pastors, John Westbrook often led the meeting. Other dorm residents, showing a modicum of respect, held the noise down to tolerable levels until all hall and shower lights went dark at 11 pm.

Suddenly two large men came running down the hall yelling at the top of their lungs.

"Whaaa-Hooo, someone finally shot that Nigger, Commie bastard!"

I jumped up to see what the commotion was about. The two doing the yelling continued down the corridor and turned into the next hallway. The halls made a large rectangle on the floor. I knew if they continued, they would return to our hallway. I could hear them on the backside of the building, continuing to yell as loud as they could. Usual horseplay of someone with too much to drink, this was not! Their voices carried a definite edge.

Several young men came to the door of their rooms or suites and looked up and down the hallways.

"What's going on?" Someone yelled.

"Beats me." Another answered. "But someone is fired up!"

We moved down to the foyer in the center of the building leading to the front steps. The mail boxes and visitors' couches filled the small square foyer at the entryway. The design was too small for much of a gathering place. Mostly we used it to get in and get out of the building or to grab the mail and go. That night it became crowded within minutes. Most of us kept our confused looks while we searched for any news. Tommy Reaux, the first black athlete to graduate Baylor and one of the biggest football players, came in and told us someone shot Martin Luther King Jr. His face was not confused, but angry. The news shocked us.

Soon the first two yellers who started the commotion, rounded the last turn, and approached the foyer. They continued yelling and whooping it up.

"Whaaa-Hooo, it's about time someone shot that Nigg..."

As soon as they saw Tommy, who stood about six feet two inches and weighed 220 pounds, they shut up and stopped running. Time and movement froze. The next few seconds became interminable. No one moved.

"We gotta go." The yellers blurted out and took off up the stairway to the second floor.

Tommy's face seethed with anger. The yellers obviously wanted nothing to do with him right then. I wondered why he let them escape the foyer. He was big enough and fast enough to catch them and beat the snot out of them. Stunned, the rest of us remained silent.

Why couldn't I say anything? I froze for a while before walking back to my room. My stomach hurt.

That night about 7 p.m. central time Martin Luther King, Jr. died at a Memphis, Tennessee, hospital of gunshot wounds sustained earlier that evening. That night's 10 p.m. prayer session in Martin Hall hosted over eighty people. The yellers did not attend.

Now the news of Robert Kennedy's death added another shock to my system. I wondered what might happen next. The world seemed upside down. Another time I might have stopped in Memphis to see the scene of Dr. King's assassination, but my mind remained on getting home and time was short.

## RFK Heads Home

The news reported President Johnson sent one of the three presidential airplanes designated as Air Force One to Los Angeles to retrieve Kennedy's body. The plane was not the same one that carried John F. Kennedy's body, his widow, and the newly-sworn-in President Johnson, from Dallas to Washington D.C. that November afternoon in 1963. Instead, the plane sent by Johnson to Los Angeles was over the Pacific with the Secretary of State, in route to a peace conference when the tragic events in Dallas occurred.

About 3:30 p.m. Central Daylight Time, I began crossing the long bridge from Memphis, Tennessee to West Memphis,

Arkansas. The sun remained high enough in the sky to make rippled reflections on the water flowing under the bridge as the mighty Mississippi River snaked its way to the Gulf of Mexico. I remember thinking that bridge might be the longest one I ever traveled.

As my car moved onto the bridge, the radio announced the plane bearing Robert Kennedy's body, became airborne from Los Angeles International Airport, headed for New York's LaGuardia Airport. I made the mental comparison of the 280 miles to Texarkana, Texas, at an average speed of sixty-five miles per hour, taking about four and a half hours, and the flight from Los Angeles to New York city, crossing the entire continent, approximately 2,800 miles, at six hundred miles per hour with the jet stream at its back, taking about the same amount of time.

As the afternoon wore on and I stopped only for gas and snacks, I made timely progress headed west across Arkansas. The news reports updated the status of the flight heading east as I made my way west. When I reached the outskirts of Little Rock, the plane was high above Colorado, and as I approached Texarkana, the plane began its descent into New York. For some reason, this dichotomy of two travel modes stuck in my mind. The plane crossed the nation using the same time it took me to cross one of its smaller states. The plane landed at LaGuardia Airport at 8:57 p.m. EDT, (7:57 p.m. CDT) as I crossed the state line into Texarkana, Texas. I still had another hour or so of daylight, so I kept driving.

Outside Paris, Texas, I found a roadside park and pulled over to rest. I drank a Dr Pepper left over from one of my gas stops and ate an apple I took off the breakfast bar at Southwestern Company's training site. Nashville seemed a million miles and days away. I marveled that I grabbed the apple earlier that same day. After walking two hundred yards up and down the roadside park to stretch my weary bones, I returned to the car and sat in the passenger seat, shifted rearward as much as possible in a VW, curled into an elongated S shape with my feet shifted to the right and my head to the left. Exhausted, I fell fast asleep.

I awoke a couple of times during the night and once got out and walked a bit to get the kinks out of my legs and back. I returned to the passenger seat after just a few minutes and resumed my slumber. As daylight crept into the car around 6 a.m., I got up, walked some more, washed up at the restroom, and headed down the road in search of breakfast. It was Friday, June 7.

## Aunt Daught

Fortified with a large cup of coffee and two sweet rolls, I soon pointed the Chuck Wagon toward Archer City and my aunt's home. Arriving at Aunt Daught's house—her real name was Margaret Ellen, but being my mother's sister and my grandmother's daughter, our family just called her Daught— around 9:30 a.m. she greeted me in her housecoat. She seemed flabbergasted to see me, but welcomed me and prepared a big breakfast of eggs, bacon, toast, and jelly. Over breakfast I brought her up to speed on my adventures and we shared our shock and sadness over the second Kennedy brother's assassination. Two large cups of coffee and a toilet break equipped me to continue my journey home. She hugged me and told me she loved me as I drove away from her house headed for Seymour and points west. About five miles down the road it occurred to me we spoke very little about my mother and family. That was not unusual for me since I usually thought of myself first and let my agenda dominate the conversation, but I thought it strange Aunt Daught did not ask anything about her sister and our family. My body and mind soon returned to urging the last few miles per hour from the VW, hoping to average 65 mph on the state roads heading to Morton. With any luck and a couple of stops for gas and the bathroom I planned to arrive mid-afternoon.

I reached Lubbock by early afternoon and wished the last sixty miles could disappear with a snap of my fingers. That did not happen, and I forced my weary bones to endure the last hour in my car. When I drove into my parent's driveway, around 3:30 p.m., Mother and my two younger sisters ran out to greet me. I was glad to see them, but delighted to exit the car after spending the last thirty-two hours there while covering over 1,000 miles.

## John and I Get Ready

After fifteen minutes of updates and hugs, I called John St. Clair to announce my presence. He came right over, and we began talking about what all we would need for our trip. No one needed to remind us we planned to leave the next morning. Luckily, John and I had experience with extended travel having spent three weeks together on a trip to the Boy Scout Jamboree in Valley Forge, Pennsylvania. John had a checklist of clothes, supplies, and gear. His stuff was ready. I needed to review my clothes, jackets, rain gear, and other necessities and set about gathering it all. I added my Ruger .22 pistol to the list. One never knew if we might need to shoot something in the wilds of Alaska, or so we imagined. After a brief discussion we headed off to buy food. We soon discovered we were the talk of the town.

We made Doss Thriftway our first stop. Truman Doss owned and operated the store. He usually nodded to folks as they came in the store, but when he saw us, he came out from his office, and greeted us warmly.

"So, y'all are headed to Alaska, huh?" His voice sounded more excited than I had ever heard. He asked us when we planned to leave, what we needed, and could he help us with anything. We rounded up some cokes, crackers, cookies, candy, and cheese. For good measure we added a case of beef stew and a case of chili. The cans added extra weight, but we knew the Pontiac could manage it. We never planned to eat steak every night, but really had no clue on how to plan meals, much less prepare them. Heating a can of stew or chili fit our skill set.

When we approached the checkout counter, Truman came from the back carrying a large box.

"I want to contribute this case of Vienna Wieners." His pronunciation used the local vernacular and sounded the way John and I spoke with the west Texas drawl. To an unfamiliar ear it sounded like: "Vigh-Enny Weenies." He went on to say they should keep all summer and we could open the cans as we needed them, especially on the road to Alaska, where he was sure very few McDonald's hamburger stands existed. John and I looked at each other, then both of us started for the mustard shelf to add to our stash. We grabbed plain yellow mustard and a spicy brown mustard to add flavor to the wieners. Truman insisted the case was on him and helped us load it into the trunk of John's 1967 Pontiac.

Truman waived as we got in the car ready to leave. He grinned from ear to ear.

"Y'all need to stop at the Malt Shop and tell Loma all about your trip. Most people in town are talking about it and if you talk to her, she'll pass the word to everyone who comes through. Good luck."

John and I looked at each other and without saying anything, John steered the car toward the Malt Shop. Months would pass before we could visit the familiar watering hole on the main drag of the town, and we could always use a chocolate malt or a cherry coke. Besides, we wanted to know what people were saying about us. This trip to Alaska made us celebrities in our own town.

When we walked into the Malt Shop, everyone turned and looked at us. Loma, the proprietor, had her hair pulled back in a bun and the ever-present apron around her waist. She came around the counter and gave us both a big hug. "Alaska, huh?" She grinned as she looked us up and down. "What can I get you?"

We sat down in one of the red, vinyl covered booths with a jukebox menu stuck to the wall at the end of the table, and ordered two cheeseburgers and cherry cokes. Loma turned to put in our order and then returned to talk. We felt comfortable in our old haunting ground from junior high and high school days.

She wanted to know when we would leave, what route we expected to take, how long a drive was it, and were our parents sure we knew what we were doing? So many questions, we did not know where to start answering, but before we said anything, one of the farmers stopped eating his supper and came over to our booth. Neither of us knew him very well, we just knew everyone called him Cap, but he acted like he knew us and started talking.

"You know, I was going to go to Alaska before the Chinks decided to push us out of Korea and my big plans got changed by a notice Uncle Sam wanted me to freeze my butt off just south of the DMZ. Of course, by the time me and McArthur got that settled, I had no time for Alaska. Just came home and went to farming." Cap spoke loud enough for the eight or ten customers to hear his story.

John and I looked at each other, but did not know what to say. He continued telling us before Korea he wanted to stake a claim in the wilderness and see if he could find gold south of Nome, Alaska. As things developed in his life, he never got the

47

chance, but he was sure proud we were going up north. We could find a gold mine up there, who knows? The serious look in his eyes made us think he meant every word of it, but we never thought about a gold mine, we just wanted the adventure of traveling to such a wild and exotic place. After regaling us with the interrupted plans for his life, he started to return to his seat, but stopped, turned back toward us. He reached into the right rear pocket of his coveralls and pulled out a worn wallet.

"Here's twenty dollars. Y'all take it and live a dream for me."

Before we could say anything, he walked away, leaving the twenty-dollar bill on the table between us. Loma smiled from behind the counter, turned and gathered our cheeseburgers and walked to our table. John and I simultaneously offered our thanks to Cap.

"Maybe if you hang around here a day or two, you can finance your trip. Everybody's excited for you and maybe living just a little vicariously through your adventure." I had known Loma most of my life and never before heard her use the word vicarious in a sentence. John and I smiled at each other, feeling proud of ourselves. We acknowledged no accomplishments to that point; we were yet to leave town, much less get to Alaska, but the new found fame felt good.

When I got home my daddy came upstairs to my room to talk. He wondered if I needed anything although we both understood it was a tad late to go shopping. He asked what route to Alaska we planned to follow. Luckily, John got advice from our contact in Anchorage. Instead of taking the Alcan or Alaska-Canada Highway from Dawson Creek, British Columbia, Canada to Anchorage, a distance of over 2,500 miles, he recommended that we reach Prince Rupert on the west coast as quickly as we could and take the Intercoastal Alaskan Ferry to Haines, Alaska. He said the paved Alaskan highway had several long distances of gravel, especially in British Columbia and the Yukon that forced slower speeds, sometimes as low as forty mph. For the two of us used to driving 70 mph or more on the flat, straight roads around home, 40 mph sounded as slow as driving in a funeral procession. The summer months also saw extensive construction and repair work that could delay travelers for hours. Going the coastal and ferry route cut over 1,000 miles of driving and usually ran smoothly. It still required joining the Alaska Highway at Haines Junction in the Yukon, but the last sections of the highway received higher maintenance and allowed faster travels. John had mapped out the route and when I saw it and the explanation, I agreed.

I cleaned and oiled my pistol and secured it in a waterproof bag. Daddy reminded me to be careful and not to take any chances with the firearm. I knew his court heard many cases where stupidity with firearms led to disastrous consequences and I took his advice to heart. He also urged me to get some sleep in that we talked until after 10 p.m. and he knew we planned to leave early the next morning. After stepping out of my room to go downstairs, I heard his footsteps returning. Thinking he wanted to caution me again about being careful, he surprised me when he said, "Thanks for stopping to see Aunt Daught."

He went on to explain something I did not know. When my grandmother became sick before her death a couple of years earlier, my Aunt Daught felt helpless to help because she lived four hours away. Unbeknownst to me, she and my mother had disagreements over treatment and care for my grandmother. This led to hard feelings and little or no communications between them for the past year or so. This explained why Daught and I barely discussed the family during our visit. It pleased me my daddy thought it a good thing I stopped to see her.

We also talked about John as a traveling companion for the trip. Daddy liked John and approved of our adventure although he took the opportunity to tell one of his favorite stories about the two of us. He reminded me of an incident only a few years before when John and I attended a football game at Texas Tech's Jones Stadium. Tech played SMU that night and because of a conflict he could not use his tickets and offered them to us. A freakish storm came up during the game, complete with tornado warnings and everything. The officials suspended the game while the teams moved to the dressing rooms for shelter. At that point, the clouds overhead looked dark and stormy, but no rain. The public address announcer cautioned everyone to take shelter under the substantial concrete stands of the stadium. John and I discussed it and decided to stay in place, after all, it was not raining.

Our parents followed the game on the radio broadcast and knew of the threatening weather. When the tornado warning came, Mr. St. Clair called daddy to discuss the situation and expressed some concern about our safety. Daddy confidently declared that we were both raised up solid, were in our late teens, and he was sure we knew enough to come in out of the rain. That assuaged Mr. St. Clair and the conversation ended.

At that same moment, John and I were standing out in the open getting drenched by a downpour. Of course, we tried to seek shelter, but by then all the concourse openings stood jammed packed and we could not push our way in. To compound the problem, where we stopped came under a steady stream of water coursing off the stadium structure. It was as though we stood under a downspout. Our situation, all self-induced, reminded me of the country song about the fellow too proud to come in from the rain.

Two hours later, when we arrived home, my daddy called Mr. St. Clair and apologized for over estimating our good sense. Our families laughed about it for years afterward. Despite that experience, daddy and Mrs. St. Clair allowed us to go to Alaska unchaperoned.

He bid me goodnight again and left me to sleep. Excited over the trip and the chance to see Hungie again in Denver left me awake for another hour or so. My excitement created a dream where I drove across the desert with no water for what seemed like hours and hours. Finally, I awoke, so relieved John and I faced no deserts on our journey north.

I awoke at 6 a.m. ready to go. This time instead of my car, which had been my home for the past week, we upgraded to a spacious Pontiac. The VW proved serviceable and economical, but tiny and not too powerful. That morning we would use all of the 380 horsepower the Pontiac V8 provided us.

# In the Land of the Midnight Sun

## Chapter 4
# The Road to the Ferry

John drove up to the front of our house at 6:45 a.m. with a big smile on his face. Saturday morning, June 8 did not exactly sneak up on us, but it sure came quickly. The Pontiac had our case of Vienna Wieners and a suitcase in the trunk. I added my suitcase and a backpack to the trunk and placed the pistol, secured in its bag, under the passenger seat. The backseat held two blankets and pillows ready for naps along the way. Mother asked if John needed anything to eat, knowing his mother took care of a good breakfast for him. He declined, but took a big hug from my mother and shook hands with daddy. Receiving the usual admonitions to be careful and write, we grinned, said our goodbyes, and jumped in the car.

Our first day took us north through the Texas Panhandle, retracing my trip of a week earlier toward Denver. The Pontiac's V8 engine hummed along, and John pushed our speed up to 70 mph on the mostly empty roads north. I remember thinking this sure beat the Chuck Wagon for speed and comfort.

We gassed up in Texline and said farewell to Texas as we crossed into New Mexico. My journal recorded $5.75 for gasoline at a Gulf station costing 39.9 cents per gallon. Our excitement remained unabated after the first three and a half hours on the road.

# Heading to Denver

The Pontiac proved its mettle as we cruised up Raton Pass, never falling below 65 mph, and crossed into Colorado in the early afternoon. John and I talked about expected stops along the way; Denver to visit Hungie and spend the night, Mammoth Hot Springs in Yellowstone to visit our friend Lem Chesher who had a summer job there and spend our second night. After that things got fuzzier because we were not sure of the miles we might cover in the following days across Idaho, Washington, into British Columbia, Canada, and on to Prince Rupert. We hoped after the first two days covering about five hundred miles each, we could up our totals to 600 or 700 miles per day. Even averaging 70 mph, the days ahead meant hours and hours of driving.

John drove to Raton, a little more than half way to Denver and I drove the rest of the way because I knew the way to Hungie's house. We figured about 200 to 250 miles each and then switching off would serve us well. Neither of us needed a nap that first day as we arrived in Denver before nightfall. I remarked how compared to the VW, the Pontiac was better on my legs and knees after five hundred miles.

Hungie and her roommates welcomed us with a steak dinner on the backyard grill. John and I managed the charcoal and the grill while the ladies prepped potato salad, corn-on-the-cob, and a peach pie for dessert. Our hosts asked questions about our plans and expressed excitement about our adventure. Hungie wanted to know how I decided to leave the Bible selling and head to Alaska and my only response was it felt right so I made a quick decision. John added he was glad of that development because he could not undertake the trip alone. We laughed and joked about a week in the car, sleeping in rest stops, and seeing new lands as we headed north and west. John, ever humble, downplayed his fishing abilities, but I touted him as our food provider. I expected him to catch fish in the lakes and rivers we saw along the way. Little did we know at that point his fishing opportunities on the trip would be very rare.

## Yellowstone

Early morning found us awake and ready to resume our travels. We enjoyed a big breakfast, two cups of coffee along with pancakes and bacon. We planned to reach Mammoth Hot Springs in Yellowstone National Park before nightfall, six hundred miles north and west of Denver. As we gathered everything together and loaded the Pontiac, I pulled Hungie aside and asked her if she would marry me sometime in the next year. It came with no thought or planning. The time was right. I had no engagement ring and we agreed to use a ring of her mother's with a big diamond. I felt a little cheap about that, but Hungie seemed thrilled. We agreed to work out the details later and John and I jumped in the car.

Clear skies and bright sunshine turned to clouds and then rain by the time we reached Rawlings, Wyoming. The grey clouds covered the sky as far as we could see to the north and the temperature kept dropping. We joked we might see snow in June and laughed at the possibility. By the time we turned west at Muddy Gap the sleet began. Our speed dropped, but we kept pushing it to the edge of recklessness. At Dubois, the snow started in earnest, but lucky for us, it melted soon after it hit the pavement. We barely averaged 60 mph for the three hours across the middle of Wyoming. At Moran we saw turnouts for sightseeing in Grand Teton National Park, but low-hanging, grey clouds and intermittent snow dominated our views. We turned north toward Yellowstone National Park and picked up plenty of traffic.

Travel trailers and recreational vehicles jammed the roads and we all slowed to about 40 mph for the next two hours. Despite craning our necks and looking out the back window, we saw no mountains. Because I visited the Tetons a few years earlier, I told John what he was missing, but neither of us wanted to wait around for clear skies. We had places to go and people to see.

We drove past Old Faithful lodge, not even considering a stop to see the geyser. I told John about the conversation my daddy and I had with the waiter at the lodge and how it planted the idea for summer adventures. I admitted Alaska was a place too far for my dreams, but now I was excited it was going to really happen.

We rolled into Mammoth Hot Springs and began looking for Lem around 8:30 p.m., thirteen and a half hours after leaving Denver and close to 30 degrees cooler than when we started. John told me if the temperatures dropped as we went north, we faced chilly days ahead. Despite the weather and the crowded roads in Grand Teton and Yellowstone National Parks, we chalked it up to a good day. Only problem came from the aches and pains born from most all day spent in the car. We traded off the driving duty and each of us took a nap for an hour or more, so we felt rested, just stiff, and achy.

Lem took us to a restaurant in Gardiner, Montana, just outside the gate to Yellowstone and we chowed down while telling Lem our travel route, expected arrival in Alaska, how we planned to catch the ferry, we carried a pistol, but did not expect to use it, and finally, asking if he could loan us some money. The last part was a long-standing joke dating back to when we spent three weeks together on that Boy Scout trip to Valley Forge. Lem and I proved fairly loose with our money, but John was beyond frugal. He often took five minutes to decide whether or not to buy a Milky Way chocolate bar. Lem and I got in the habit of asking if he could spare a little for us, but he usually ignored us. John and I turned the tables this time as I joined John in asking Lem, who now had a steady job, if he could spare something for us to spend on our adventure north. At first Lem seemed to seriously consider making us a loan, but before we could crack a grin, he caught on and told us to cut it out.

We enjoyed the visit and Lem got us settled into a campground around 10 p.m. He shared a small cabin with three others and had no room for visitors, even those willing to sleep on the floor. The snow stopped, but it was cold outside, and we did not want to take the chance of sleeping outside. John took the front seat, and I took the back. We said our goodbyes and apologized for the short visit. Lem wished us well and returned to his cabin while we hoped to sleep some before daylight. Another long day lay ahead of us.

In a small town like Morton, Texas, everyone knows everyone else, so most of our lives to that point were among people we knew, recognized, and greeted on the street. John mentioned after seeing Lem, we might not see anyone we knew for the rest of the summer. I told him I knew my cousin in Spokane, Washington and hoped to see her, but other than her, he spoke the truth.

Because of the cramped sleeping arrangement, neither of us slept well. We woke up before dawn. I went to the men's toilet and when I got back John was awake and ready to go. We figured we could be uncomfortable with the car moving as much as trying to go back to sleep. We drove onto the highway before 5:30 a.m. headed for Idaho and Washington, where my cousin, Aunt Daught's daughter Ceil, lived with her family. I called her from Denver and said we might come through and she insisted we stop to visit. We hoped to cover the 482 miles by early afternoon and the quick start that morning helped.

Getting away from Yellowstone and all the tourist traffic helped as we picked up the pace across western Montana and the panhandle of Idaho. After hitting Interstate 90 at Livingston, Montana, we drove 75 and 80 mph for long stretches. We both scanned the horizon, rest stops, and bridge overpasses for Montana and Idaho troopers, but saw very few, and when we did our speed dropped to the 65 or 70 mph limits. The green valleys, rivers, and forests looked nothing like the west Texas plains we left behind.

## My Cousin in Spokane

We called ahead and my cousin had a luncheon prepared for us by the time we reached Spokane. Her husband and three kids asked hundreds of questions about our trek, and we felt a little like celebrities talking big about Alaska and our plans. With a satisfying meal of sandwiches, potato chips, and iced tea under our belts we headed off for Grand Coulee Dam. We spent just over an hour in Spokane and hoped to reach the Canadian border before we stopped for the day.

We crossed over the Grand Coulee Dam and stopped just long enough to take in the mighty Columbia River dammed behind it and below it, snaking its way to the Pacific ocean. It seemed the dam held enough concrete to cover all of Cochran County, Texas. It was quite a sight. By the time we left Grand Coulee Dam we had accumulated just under six hundred miles for the day. The 4:30 p.m. hour left us with another three to three and a half hours of daylight and the border only lay two hours and one hundred miles away. We wasted no time dropping off the high desert plateau of eastern Washington down to Omak where we turned north to Canada.

At Osoyoos, British Columbia, Canada, just inside the border we stopped for gas and found ourselves in a different land. First thing we discovered dealt with gasoline. The pump listed liters, not gallons and we thought the gas tank might explode when the meter passed twenty, what we thought meant gallons. We usually took 16 to 18 gallons and did not understand how we got over twenty gallons in there. We thought the price looked cheap but figured Canada must have a gas war. We felt pleased about getting gasoline at 14.5 cents per gallon. John's good, practical sense brought him to examine the meter and he informed me about the liters not gallons switch. By the time the sale totaled, we fully understood no gas war existed. When the attendant converted our U.S. dollars to Canadian dollars, we spent about 10% more for a full tank than back in the good ole U.S.A. The vagaries of travel began to sink into our small town, unsophisticated brains as we prepared to continue further into Canada.

We asked the attendant how far it was to Cache Creek. We saw it on the map and thought we could reach it before nightfall. Of course, we figured things in miles and the Canadians figured in kilometers. Turned out miles and kilometers were not the biggest problem. Neither of us understood Cache was a French word, and of course we had no way of knowing the correct pronunciation was like money; "cash." Our west Texas drawl and labored pronunciations came out sounding like "catch-ee creek." The fellow gave me a bewildered look when I asked about the distance to "catch-ee creek," so John came over and tried his luck. More confused looks from the gas station guy. The man spoke with a distinct accent, we just did not know what kind of accent, and it dawned on us his brain could not discern our words. We tried other ways to say the destination, but they brought more dazed looks. Finally, before we thought of returning to the car and bringing the map to show the fellow, he said, "It is a long ways to Kansas City."

# Hellfire, we knew that!

After retrieving the map and showing the spot, we learned how to say Cache Creek. The attendant was French Canadian, so his accent did not help us much, but when he saw it on the map, a broad grin came across his face, and he repeated; "cash, cash, cash." Of course when he continued by saying it lay about three hundred kilometers away, we looked as confused to him as he did to us earlier. Deciding to do our own calculations, we noted the three hundred kilometers and climbed back into the Pontiac headed for Cache Creek. John's math aptitude and good sense revealed it was 'only' 186 miles.

# Travels in British Columbia

We made it to a rest stop outside Ashcroft, B.C., where Cache Creek joins the Thompson River a few miles south of the town of Cache Creek. We later learned the Thompson River joins the Fraser River downstream and eventually ends up in Vancouver, B.C., but by nearly 10 p.m. we were too exhausted to care how close or far we were from the Pacific Ocean. We camped beside the car and slept outdoors. Thank goodness for my cousin feeding us earlier that afternoon because after that meal we only partook of cokes, potato chips, and candy bars. We held the Vienna Wieners in reserve, thinking we might need them once we got to the wilderness. John had no time or interest for fishing.

Our journey that day covered over 850 miles and we found ourselves deep into the sparsely populated wilderness of western Canada. We felt good about our progress and fell sound asleep without any conversation. Covering that many miles in one day took the edge off our excitement.

Sleeping outside in a sleeping bag in an unfamiliar place, even with cool, clean air, does not lend itself to lengthy periods of good, sound sleeping. Sleep that night never reached long intervals. We awoke every hour or so at an unfamiliar noise or other travelers pulling into the rest stop. When the dawn broke around 5 a.m., we loaded up and headed into Cache Creek for breakfast. Both of us kept saying 'cash, cash, cash," as if we became sophisticated Francophiles overnight.

It was Tuesday, June 11, the beginning of our fourth day on the road.

At Clinton, B.C., we added fifty-five liters to the gas tank and kept rolling. We hoped to reach Prince Rupert, on the west coast, seven hundred miles, not kilometers, away by evening. It marked the end of the Alaska Maritime Highway and the southern terminus of the Alaska Ferry system. That destination required another long day in the car, but we were up for it.

The countryside changed from the semi-arid plateau of eastern Washington state in the U.S. To our west we saw the Pacific Coast Mountains which extended from southwestern Yukon, through the Alaska Panhandle and south along the coast of British Columbia to the Fraser River mouth at Vancouver. The range included volcanic and non-volcanic mountains with extensive ice fields which became visible the further north we drove. The snowcapped and ice bound peaks gave us sights never seen before and heightened our excitement about being far from home.

The peaks ranged from 12,000 to 13,000 feet but because of their proximity to the coast and sea level, they seemed much more prominent than the Rocky Mountains of Colorado, which rise from a 5,000-foot base. As we drove along the eastern edge of the mountains, we saw the uplift to the west where the dry interior plateau gave way to the boreal forest and the heavily glaciated peaks of the Coastal Mountains. The further north we drove the heavier the forests. We looked at each other and grinned at the beautiful sights as we drove through unfamiliar, at least to our experience, lands.

We continued north past Williams Lake and Quesnel toward Prince George. There we made, or confirmed, our decision to head for the ferry instead of going to the Alcan Highway. We faced the choice of turning northeast toward Dawson Creek, B.C., the southern end of the highway, but eschewed that route with the expectation the ferry would allow us to cover more distance in a shorter time.

We grabbed gas station sandwiches, more soft drinks and chips, and another full tank of gasoline in Prince George. Our legs had stiffened considerably so we walked around and around the gas station trying to limber up a bit before we again folded ourselves into the Pontiac. We noticed the further we got from the states, the more expensive the gasoline, whether in liters or in gallons. We began to long for the hometown prices for gasoline made from West Texas crude. The pump prices confirmed we found ourselves a long way from the Permian Basin oil fields of our home and the attendant cheap gasoline.

At Prince George, we turned west leaving the Fraser River valley and headed higher along the eastern flank of the mountains toward Fort Fraser and Houston. Houston, B.C. proved to be only a wide spot in the road, much different than the Houston, Texas it brought to our minds. The elevation rose as we got into increasingly forested areas.

The road proved excellent, only a few construction delays, and although narrower than the roads in Cochran County, Texas, allowed room for passing travel trailers and recreation vehicles. We spent one span of twenty minutes or so behind a string of such tourists, but mostly kept to speeds between 60 and 70 miles per hour, or 90 and 110 kilometers per hour. Going one hundred kph seemed much faster, but after a while the novelty wore off and we realized speed was speed whether measured in miles per hour or kilometers per hour. We went back to keeping track in miles per hour.

At Houston, B.C. we noticed the snow-covered mountains lay much closer and the weather cooled considerably. A steady afternoon shower slowed us a bit, but the pine-scented air after the fresh rain, sure smelled good. The temperature hovered in the high fifty's to low 60's Fahrenheit and even though we knew Canada used a Celsius scale, we kept track the way we knew. If we passed a sign on a building with a temperature reading of 18 degrees, we just looked at each other and said it seemed warmer to us rather than trying to figure out what it meant in Fahrenheit. Hey, we adapted as we could along the way.

We continued on to New Hazelton for another gas stop. It presented a peculiar situation in that New Hazelton, along Highway 16, lay within two miles of Hazleton, and within one mile of South Hazelton. Judging from our observations, the three towns combined could not hold more than 1,500 souls. We wondered aloud how so few people could not agree on one name for the general location, but insisted on three names.

After the stop, John asked me if I had seen anyone I knew that day. I admitted I had not, and added this may be the first of many days when we go without seeing anyone we knew.

There we picked up the Skeena River, a river neither of us heard of before, which carried more water at a faster pace than we could remember from any other rivers. Keep in mind we had little experience with rivers at all and water flowing at such a rate made quite an impression on us. John remarked how a river running that swiftly made for difficult fishing and we bemoaned how our plan for fishing along the way proved elusive. Four days into our journey and John was yet to wet a hook. We might have enjoyed the trip and the scenery if we took more time and allowed for fishing, but we remained determined to put as many miles between us and Texas as we could in as short a time as possible.

## Prince Rupert and the Dump

We followed the Skeena River valley, increasingly surrounded by higher and higher mountains, down to the coast at Prince Rupert. The pine forest amazed us. There were more trees within one hundred yards of the road than existed in the entire county where we spent all our lives up to that point. The only trees at home came as a result of someone wanting them, planting them, and nurturing them. Here in British Columbia, we could not begin to count all the trees.

As we approached the coast, we wondered about the ferry schedule and how to find the port. Driving into the town we realized the only road in was about the only road, period. We drove to the end of the road and found the sign for the Alaska Ferry terminal.

We read all the pertinent information on the bulletin board at the terminal and discussed our options. The posted schedule listed a 9:00 a.m. departure time for the ferry northbound to Haines, Alaska. The next few sentences cautioned cars without reservations, which we had none, would board on a first-come, first-served basis after all reserved spots boarded. Fare for a car between eleven feet and twenty feet in length totaled $96.00 Canadian. Passenger fares came in addition to vehicles and the cost from Prince Rupert to Haines came to $33.25 Canadian, each. A cabin with berths for sleeping on the lowest level, cost another $8.50 per person. A sleeping berth sounded good to our weary bones, so we decided to add the added cost in hopes of catching up on our sleep. We gulped a bit at the cost, and I told

John we did not come all this way to save money, and besides, what options did we have. But the cost was not our main concern. Getting on the ferry was priority number one.

Only one departure per day made it imperative we get the Pontiac on the ferry the next morning. Lacking a reservation made us anxious about how many cars held reservations. If we missed this one, we faced a day in Prince Rupert sitting around waiting for the next ferry and we needed to be in Anchorage as soon as possible. The port listed the carrying capacity for the MV Matanuska, the ferry docked at the port, as 128 cars and five hundred passengers. We saw a dozen or so travel trailers and recreation vehicles at a couple of parking lots in town and wondered if a car pulling a travel trailer counted as two vehicles. We did not see five hundred people anywhere in town, but we did arrive after dark so we could not be certain. At any rate we dedicated ourselves to being in line as soon as possible for the next morning's queuing. A sign in oversized letters cautioned that no one could join the queue, reservations or not, more than two hours before departure. That meant 7 a.m., but we planned to be there waiting to get in line well before 7. We saw the lanes leading to the dock and presumed cars would fill them early the next morning. One of the lanes had markings for reservations, but the other two lanes had no markings.

The schedule listed the next ferry as including Sitka, Alaska, for one of the ports of call. That added another ten hours to the trip to Haines, putting the ferry in there 48 hours and 652 miles after leaving Prince Rupert. This meant we could resume the driving part into the Yukon and Alaska, early Friday morning. Knowing we reached at least half way to our destination made us proud, but we found ourselves too exhausted to celebrate.

We wanted to sleep somewhere close, but lacked any ideas for a spot nearby. Nightfall came two hours earlier, but the western sky still carried hints of light. We turned the car toward the small village to see if any establishments remained open. We drove only a couple of blocks and saw a sign saying, "Prince Rupert Public Waste Dump," and a dirt road heading southeast of the port. John looked at me and asked if I had ever slept in a dump before. I shook my head from shoulder to shoulder saying, "No," and said, "But this could be the first time."

We followed the road less than fifty yards until it stopped at the edge of a huge pile of garbage and refuse. The car lights showed only trash as far up the hill as we could see. No people, no cars, and no more signs. One light pole stood back at the entrance, but nothing lit our area. We took that as permission to camp and got out of the car. Not wanting to wander too far from the car, we pitched our sleeping bags on the driver's side and after taking a stop twenty yards away to relieve ourselves, we stretched out on the ground. We talked a bit about wolves, bears, or other wildlife coming for us in the night and I retrieved my pistol from under the car seat just in case. We noticed a slightly unpleasant odor wafting across us and our sleeping bags, but found ourselves too tired to complain, much less get up and seek other accommodations.

As one might imagine, we spent a fitful night. Anxious about arriving early at the port and, sleeping in a dump, caused us to wake every hour or less and check the time and our wellbeing. After looking around and convinced we could sleep more, we dozed off for another brief period before repeating the routine. We noticed less and less of the unpleasant odor in the early morning hours, but we attributed it to our noses adjusting to the environment. By 4:00 a.m. as light began creeping over the hillside to the east, we got up and drove the short distance to the ferry port. Neither of us mentioned the smell as we drove away. One RV beat us there, but we slapped high fives at being the second car in the lot awaiting the official opening, still three hours away.

Our spirits rose as we calculated our chances of getting onboard; surely the reservation line would not include 126 vehicles.

At 7 a.m. an attendant came out of the terminal and asked if we had a reservation. He motioned for us to get in the open lane with no markings. We were the first in that line. Turned out only eight cars had reservations, so we joined the ferry as the ninth car to board. The Canadian custom folks only looked at our drivers' licenses before directing us onto the ramp leading into the garage part of the ship, near the water line. Good thing because we had no passports. We gave thanks for the friendly Canadians not requiring one.

Once on board, we found our sleeping berths, deep in the bowels of the ship, and returned to the snack bar for coffee and sweet rolls. A light rain textured the deck outside the snack bar, and we settled in for two days aboard the MV Matanuska, named for a glacier outside Palmer, Alaska. We felt good about being on the ferry without a delay and no one asked why we smelled like a dump.

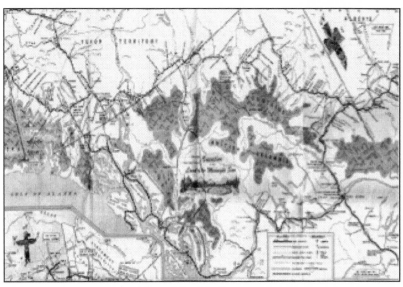

Map of Inside Passage,
"The Milepost" 1968 Edition

# Chapter 5
# Inside Passage to Haines

The ferry loaded efficiently, blew the horn exactly at 9 a.m., and slowly pulled away from the dock at Prince Rupert. Next stop, Ketchikan, Alaska. The rain continued but the cruise included some unexpected turns.

The Captain's voice came over the loud speaker saying the ferry would be in Canadian waters for two hours before passing into Alaskan waters near 54° 40' latitude. We had no idea where that was on the globe, but knew it was further north than either of us had ever been. He also mentioned there were no custom checks until we left the ferry at our destination.

After breakfast we toured the ship and hustled in from the rain each time we ventured out onto one of the decks. Luckily, there were observation windows along each side of the ship for viewing, but the low cloud deck and the rain offered little hope for sightseeing. By mid-morning we looked at each other, nodded our heads at the same time, and headed to the sleeping berths. The combination of days on the road and sleeping in a trash dump took its toll on our bodies. Both of us fell asleep in minutes.

Traveling 2,700 miles in four days, averaging 787 miles the last two days, and sleeping on the ground or in the car three of the nights, exhausted us. We also lacked good nutrition along the way and long days with little sleep allowed weariness to overcome both of us. The sleeping berths came without any extra  frills; single bunks suspended from the wall by chains and mattresses thinner than the cheapest dorm at Baylor. John and I both stood over 6-foot-tall, and the bunks seemed designed for someone five foot ten inches at most; almost, but not long enough for us to stretch out. It made no difference to us. The accumulated fatigue caused us to sleep as soon as we got in the bunks.

Charlie aboard the ferry,
MV Matanuska

## Getting Sleep

We cannot tell you what Ketchikan or Wrangell, Alaska looked like because we slept through both ports of call. I awoke in the early evening as we pulled into Petersburg. The rain stopped, but the clouds hung low over the mountains. Lush, green fir and pine trees covered the mountainsides that came right down to the water's edge. No roads anywhere in sight along the shoreline except one main street headed into Petersburg. Daylight remained even though it was past 10 p.m. The grey, low hanging clouds dulled any illumination from the remaining daylight.

I walked out on deck to look around and saw the stevedores and dock workers working efficiently to load and unload cargo destined for Petersburg. No vehicles joined us, and the ship soon pulled away from the dock and headed for Sitka. Sleeping during the day kept me awake as the ferry slid through the dark waters between the mainland and the islands dotting the coastline. The waters took on a dark greenish-blue color as we turned west toward the Pacific ocean.

Sitka lies on the western side of Baranof Island, named for the early Russian explorer and settler in the area. It looks out into a vast expanse of the northern Pacific ocean to the west and the Gulf of Alaska to the northwest. It marked the only port facing the open water of the Pacific along the ferry's route. All other stops came within the waterways between the coast and the islands. Long before we came along, the explorers called this the 'Inside Passage," because of its sheltered route protected by the chain of islands. No roads served the town, only the ferry and airplane service delivered people and goods to the former capital of the territory. I remained wide awake even though we reached the dock in Sitka in the middle of the night. The laborers repeated their efficient on and off-loading service and the ferry did not linger in the port.

In the early hours of the morning we returned to our bunks and quickly fell asleep. Our long naps did not replenish our bodies' needed rest. Our exhaustion allowed six added hours of sleep before we woke mid-morning and headed for the snack bar for breakfast. The ferry sailed at a steady, but not too speedy pace, for the expected arrival in Juneau by early afternoon. It was Thursday, June 13.

The clouds continued to fit snugly against the mountains, obscuring their tops, but a few patches of blue appeared and then soon hid from us as we continued north toward Juneau. After our meal we went out on deck to take in the environment. Only six or eight folks took places along the rails, most sat in deck chairs back closer to the large windows separating the outside decks from the lounge, snack bar, and observation areas. We took deck chairs on the port side and began looking at the fertile forests blanketing the hillsides. Occasionally, we spotted snow or ice toward the top of the mountains, but most remained hidden by the cloud layer.

## The Birders

In the deck chairs next to us sat an older couple, each holding a pair of binoculars. They looked back and forth along the coastline, drank coffee from a thermos, talked constantly with each other, and from time-to-time jotted down notes in a spiral notebook. Both came prepared with rain gear, heavy sweaters, gloves, and hats. John and I shivered a bit with our long-sleeved shirts and light sweaters and envied these folks' obvious comfort despite the cool, wet air. I wondered what they found so interesting. Looking in the direction they pointed their binoculars I saw twenty or thirty large birds nesting in the trees along the banks. At times the birds swooped in long, low glidepaths barely above the water level. The birds looked large, but were too far away for me to identify them. Curious, I started a conversation with the lady seated next to me.

"We are birders." She explained, although I was unfamiliar with the term. My puzzled look led her to explain they considered themselves serious bird watchers and they booked the ferry trip months ago so they could see the bald eagles along the coast. Her husband was a professor at the University of Wisconsin in Madison in the ornithology department of the College of Animal Sciences. She too was a professor, of Russian literature, but joined her husband on trips to see birds. She continued by telling me 1968 was a "Big Year" for them. In bird watching parlance that meant they wanted to see, identify, and count as many species of birds as possible during the year. They noted each species and added it to their year list, national list, and lifetime lists. Her knowledge and enthusiasm for birds surprised me. I learned more about birds in the following fifteen minutes than I did the first twenty-one years of my life.

My bird watching lesson continued as she informed me over 10,000 bird species existed across the globe. Her lifetime list included over 2,000 and her husband's over 3,500. It occurred to me I might list twenty birds if I created such a list and all would be unexciting: robins, sparrows, quail, doves, maybe a hawk or two. I could not remember seeing a bald eagle in a zoo, much less in the wild.

Eagle near Mendenhall Glacier

The ferry ride headed north along the Inside Passage and presented an ideal trip for their Big Year. They came specifically to see bald eagles and osprey. Alaska was home to more bald eagles than any other state and southeast Alaska dominated the state's eagle population. I learned the bald eagle went on the endangered species list the year before and authorities worried the nation's symbol could go extinct. She talked about how scientists suspected a pesticide, DDT, had a deleterious effect on the reproduction of bald eagles. Wildlife officials thought the osprey population faced the same issue. Fish dominated the diets of both eagles and osprey and passed along the toxins to the birds.

I got a quick science lesson on biomagnification, the increased concentration of toxins, such as pesticides, in the tissue of organisms within the eagles' food chain. This led to interference with the bird's ability to produce calcium, making the bird either sterile or unable to lay healthy eggs. Since eagles mate for life, breeding pairs so affected become unable to generate future generations. This resulted in the decline in the number of bald eagles. The birder couple wanted to see as many eagles as they could before the population dropped further. Little did I know before this, but the lady informed me southeast Alaska, especially along the Inside Passage, had more breeding pairs of bald eagles than all the lower forty-eight states combined.

Displaying her passion for the bald eagle, she continued to tell me about the birds. She related how they are the largest of the raptors, their size dwarfing the Turkey Vulture and Red-tailed Hawks. They soar with long, broad wings flattened out to catch the wind and air currents. They also swoop very low over the sea taking prey by surprise. Observers often see the eagles as scavengers, sometimes stealing fish from ospreys, or landing on the ground to feed on carrion. She also mentioned they are not bald, but have white head feathers that, from a distance made them appear bald to early observers, and the name stuck with them. The lady proved to be a veritable Eagle Encyclopedia.

The lady graciously asked if I wanted a look through the binoculars and extended a large, almost foot-long object toward me. The eye pieces held rubber eye cups to allow the viewer to pull the binoculars up against the brow. The other end where the light came into the instrument measured at least two- and one-half inches in diameter. The weight surprised me, but the view it allowed surprised me even more. The eagles in the treetops were easy to see, but those flying required patience and skill. The enhanced magnification caused me to lose sight of the flying birds. It took ten or so minutes before I could follow one of the swooping eagles with a steady hand. The birds flew effortlessly and seemed to glide over the water with little effort before banking and heading higher. I wished to see an eagle grab a fish out of the water with its talons, but I never did. After twenty minutes or so I began to feel guilty about hogging all the time with the binoculars and returned them with my thanks. The lady smiled and despite my wishing she might urge me to keep them, quickly put the strap over her head and resumed watching.

We continued steadily moving up the channel toward Juneau. The ornithology professor offered that the Mendenhall glacier would be visible after we passed Juneau and the area offered dozens of eagles. He urged us to return to the starboard deck to view more eagles as we passed the glacier. Seeing a glacier sounded cool to me and the added bonus of more eagles heightened the already high excitement of our voyage. Getting rest and much needed sleep put us in a great mood to enjoy the rest of the day. The eagles were an added bonus.

## Juneau

Juneau's stop came around 5 p.m. with no sign evening approached. The sunlight, even covered by the heavy clouds, made it seem much earlier. We began to realize the lengthening hours of sunlight as we made our way north. The longest day of the year remained days away, but we took note of how long the daylight lingered. Juneau lay just above 58° North of the equator and the ship's daily bulletin listed sunrise as 3:51a.m. and sunset at

10:04 p.m. That gave us another five hours before sunset and six before full darkness.

For a state's capital, Juneau did not offer much. We saw one multistory building, but the rest of the town lay snugly against the shoreline and only two or three city blocks deep. The town presented much more length down the coastline than it did depth into the mainland. In the 1960 census Juneau recorded 7,500 hardy souls as residents. We cruised by the main part of town and fourteen miles north to Auke Bay where the ferries to and from Sitka docked. The ship slowed for ten miles before and along the coast near the town. We docked at the port along the appropriately named, Glacier Highway because the dock allowed a fine view of the face of Mendenhall Glacier only two miles inland. We got our first close up look at a glacier from there.

Mendenhall Glacier extends northwest up the Mendenhall valley joining the Juneau Icefield about eight miles up the valley. Research scientists monitored the outlet glaciers of the Juneau Icefield, including Mendenhall, beginning in 1942. On the west side of the valley, the terminus of the Mendenhall Glacier retreated 1 3/4 miles since 1929 when the ice melt created Mendenhall Lake. Estimates indicated a retreat over two and a half miles since the mid-1700's when explorers visited the region. The lake resulted from the run-off from the glacier and increased in size as the glacier pulled back. The resulting lake created a unique ecosystem of fresh water and became a nursery for several varieties of fish including salmon, Dolly Varden, char and cutthroat trout. That in turn, created more food for the bald eagles and osprey.

As the professor predicted, we saw dozens of bald eagles and osprey filling the sky and treetops near the port.

Having no knowledge or clue about retreating or advancing glaciers, John and I agreed the Mendenhall Glacier represented the biggest hunk of ice we ever saw. John wished we had time for him to try his luck with the fish in the lake, but lands still farther north called to us.

The ferry stayed longer in Juneau loading and unloading cargo than the earlier ports. We guessed the capital needed more supplies than the smaller towns along the way. Juneau, like Sitka, received access only by air and sea. No roads from there joined any highway system in Alaska or Canada, making the ferry a vital part of commerce in the region. Coming from a farm and ranch country served by farm-to-market and state roads, John and I realized how vastly different Juneau was from Morton. The remoteness, the glaciers, the coastline, and the eagles all told us we were not in West Texas anymore.

After two hours in port at Juneau we resumed sailing the Inside Passage toward its northern-most ports of Haines and Skagway. We pulled away from the dock around 7 p.m. for the 11 ½ hour journey on to Haines. That presented our last chance to stretch out in a bunk before getting back in the Pontiac and resuming our drive. We planned to camp along the way for the next couple of nights, but long days in the car remained ahead of us.

We learned another fact of earth science from the birder professors onboard. We talked with them about the usual stuff: where we lived, where we went to school, and our earlier travels. I mentioned working in the Rocky Mountains of Colorado the previous summer and told them of riding horseback to the top of the Continental Divide. That led to a discussion about the vagaries of what folks call the tree line or timberline, the elevation at which trees no longer grew. Above certain elevations the lack of moisture and cold temperatures prevented tree growth. They knew the tree line in Colorado came between 11,000 and 12,00 feet above sea level and asked about trees and birds along the divide in Colorado. I admitted I saw blue jays and hawks in Colorado, but did not recall any birds along the divide. The man mentioned how the tree line in the Canadian Rockies around 51° North latitude lay about 7,900 feet above sea level, but there in southeast Alaska, nearing 60° North, the tree line dropped to between 1,500 and 2,000 feet. He told us to watch how quickly above sea level the trees disappeared when we got to the Chugach Mountains around Anchorage. I guess he appeared a bit pedantic because John imitated him with an almost mocking tone when we retreated to the cabin. "Of course, you know the tree line drops in elevation as you move north," he added as though I missed the earlier lecture. We laughed about learning something every day.

Before we called it a night, John also asked if I saw anyone I knew during the day. I had not.

Soon we fell asleep thinking of getting in the car and pushing to Anchorage. With the sunrise in Haines coming at 3:36 a.m. we needed to sleep while it remained dark. We figured two, maybe two and a half days lay ahead of us.

We woke at 6:00 a.m., gathered our clothes and personal items and went down to the garage level to deposit them in the Pontiac. Snack bar for coffee and donuts came next in that we remained half an hour out of Haines. At the snack bar we found lots of blue sky and puffy clouds for a morning with the sun higher in the sky than one expected that early.

The ferry slid through the water headed north up the Lynn Canal, the wide body of water between the mainland and a peninsula jutting into Glacier Bay. The land on both sides had snow-capped mountains which sloped steeply into the inlets and bays along the way. Just west of our route lay Glacier Bay National Monument, the sight of early explorations by Captain George Vancouver from Great Britain and George Cooper and John Muir of the U.S. All gave glowing reports of the beautiful bays and glaciers dominating the area. Partly as a result of Cooper and

Muir's lobbying, the area received a National Monument designation in 1925. Vancouver in the 1790's reported the bay almost completely covered with one glacier, but by the time Muir arrived in a canoe a century later, he found the glacier retreating up the bay as much as a mile a year. After we passed that way, President Carter, in 1980 signed the bill naming Glacier Bay as a National Park.

# End of the Ferry

As we pulled into the combined Haines/Port Chilkoot towns and dock the passengers headed to their vehicles for unloading and joining the Haines Cutoff highway north to join the Alaska Highway into the Yukon and again into Alaska. The only remaining port of call was Skagway, eight miles up the fjord, but we too, were ready to disembark. A trip to Skagway and a visit to the jumping off spot for the Klondike gold rush of the 1890's would have to wait for another day.

Anxious to get on the road, we followed the other passengers to the cars. Despite getting into the car and feeling the ferry bump into the dock before settling in, we found the crew in no hurry to let the vehicles drive off. Instead cargo containers and large pallets of boxes moved via forklifts and motorized dollies to the dock. We saw the huge ramp for the vehicles stay in its upright position and wondered why people took second place to cargo.

We sat patiently for at least half an hour before one of the drivers ahead of us got out and approached a crew member. Walking back to his car, he stopped and told us the U.S. Customs and Immigration Office in Haines, a required stop before entering Alaska from Canada, did not open until 8 a.m., and all vehicles needed clearance before debarkation. Even though we made stops in ports of call in Alaska before Haines, we remained onboard so our official point of origin for the ferry was Prince Rupert, which just happened to be in another country. Dang, the hour and a half wait seemed to take forever, partly because of the government bureaucracy and partly because of our desire to hit the road. Finally, at 7:30 the crew let us drive off the ferry and queue up for the customs inspection. We reached our turn with the customs officials around 8:20 and received a perfunctory quizzing and inspection. The man barely looked at our Texas driver's licenses and asked us our destination before officially waiving us into Alaska. John reminded me this was the first time our feet, or in this case, the Pontiac's tires, landed on Alaskan soil.

Checking out the twin towns took no time at all. Haines/Port Chilkoot combined showed a population of maybe six hundred folks. Even our small hometown of 3,000 people looked huge by comparison to these small burgs along the Inside Passage. We filled the gas tank, bought cokes, candy bars, and bananas. The bananas carried a hefty price of fifty cents each, but we splurged, partly from the novelty of having a fresh banana that far north. We inquired about road conditions and what to expect as we headed north the 159 miles to join the Alaska Highway at Haines Junction. We neglected to ask the attendant how far it was to Kansas City or Cache Creek.

We said goodbye to the Inside Passage and felt energized by two full nights' sleep. The Pontiac seemed bigger than when we loaded it onto the ferry at Prince Rupert, but we agreed that came from 48 hours walking around or sleeping in a bunk instead of 12 to 15 hours a day in the car. John took the wheel as we left Haines and I settled into the passenger seat.

The snow-capped peaks looming on both sides of the road led us to guess on their elevation. We noticed the tree lines up the mountain sides lay within easy viewing of the road. Our guesstimate of elevation came to 3,500 feet, but they sure looked higher than that to us.

Loose gravel, not pavement, greeted us as we drove. The gas station attendant recommended 40 to 45 miles per hour on the road because flying gravel could do damage to vehicles. He also informed us their main sawmill burned a year before and temporary saw mills dotted the road for the next fifty miles or so. With the saw mills came trucks loaded with logs, dust and gravel thrown into the air, and both meant slower going than we planned. The last thing we needed was a busted windshield resulting from gravel thrown by logging trucks. We looked at each other with disappointment at the news, but confirmed the conditions merited caution.

Ordinarily, these developments would have dampened our excitement, but we had arrived in Alaska and remained so excited to reach the Yukon and Anchorage. We grinned at each other as we drove away from Haines at 45 mph.

Charlie with his pipe
enters the Yukon Territory

# Chapter 6
# The Yukon & Tok

Our grand plans of making a speedy trip from Haines to Anchorage met obstacles along the next section of the road. The gravel road slowed us more than we wanted, but we also met other delays and aggravations. Getting to and through the Yukon Territory took longer than we expected.

At the edge of town we turned north along the Chilkat River estuary. The river runs into the northern Pacific ocean via the Chilkat Arm at the head of the Lynn Canal, the longest fjord in North America. The mountains rose quickly on each side and lush, green pine forests blanketed the hillside. The sunshine welcomed us back on the road. Our excitement buoyed us for the miles ahead.

At mile marker 42.2 the Canadian Customs and Immigration office, a small, one-story building with a tin roof, sat off to the side of the road. The road split into two lanes with a few rubber cone barriers designating lanes leading to a stop sign for each one. Only one vehicle per lane could pass as an officer stood next to each stop sign. The two officers stood at the driver's side of the vehicles. Lucky for us, the office was open and doing business with several cars in line. We took our place in line, three cars back and waited. The officials spent an inordinate amount of time with each vehicle, but did not hold any of the cars ahead of us. After what seemed to us as a longer than necessary time, the officers waived the cars through. As the car ahead of us pulled back onto the highway, John drove up to the barrier and rolled down his window.

"Good morning, gentlemen." The officer started innocently enough but we soon found out he had lots of questions.

"Where are you headed?"

"Anchorage." Our reply. The officer looked at me for several seconds, but said nothing more. He turned back to John and asked how much money we carried with us. Although we thought it strange, we looked at each other and then responded, "A couple hundred dollars, American." He looked unimpressed although it seemed like plenty of cash to us. I wondered why he cared what money we carried.

"Do you mind showing me?" The officer continued looking at John. We later guessed the puzzled looks on our faces led him to a story he obviously used with travelers. He informed us every day they get travelers who say Alaska is their destination but do not have sufficient money to get them through British Columbia and the Yukon. He mentioned how they end up camping in illegal spots along the road and try to make it on fishing and hunting. At some point the Royal Canadian Mounted Police escort them, not exactly arrested, but forced to move into a nearby village. He added that often the nearest village had few facilities or amenities. He went on to say the Canadian government was generous with those in need, but cannot feed, house, and return to their home states, foolhardy travelers who run out of money somewhere in the Yukon.

We did not think we fit the foolhardy description, but we both reached into our back pockets and pulled out our wallets. John first opened his wallet to show several bills. This led the officer to turn his head toward me. I showed him four twenty-dollar bills, a couple of five-dollar bills, and a ten or two. He nodded his head showing we passed the money test. We thought he would waive us through, but we began to understand why the line of cars ahead of us moved so slowly as the officer continued the interview.

## The Hidden Pistol

"Are you carrying any firearms?"

John looked at me knowing I had the Ruger pistol in a bag under my seat.

"Are firearms not allowed in Canada?" I asked, trying to sound as innocent as possible.

"Yes, but they must remain sealed in a plastic case or bag with a customs stamp for as long as you remain in Canada. We don't want people hunting alongside the road."

"What about fishing?" John asked, giving me a second to collect my thoughts. The officer indicated fishing required a license and asked if we wanted to buy a three-day fishing license. John declined the invitation.

Before answering about the firearm question, I looked over my left shoulder and saw at least eight cars behind us in the customs lane. I decided on impulse to take a chance. The officer resumed looking at me.

"No." I looked him directly in the eye as I answered and hoped he accepted it. If he insisted on searching the car, he would have caught me because, not expecting this questioning, I made no effort to conceal the pistol. It was not in an unobstructed view, but anyone would see it if they looked under my seat. I felt a queasy rumble in my stomach.

An achingly long interval passed, maybe five seconds, but it seemed longer to me. John refused to look at me and stared directly ahead. I continued to look directly at the officer. He finally nodded, stamped our entry papers, and motioned us to go ahead. John stuck the stamped entry folder above the driver's side visor and drove away. The only sound in the car besides the low growl of the tires on the gravel was a huge sigh of relief as we drove away.

"What were you thinking?" John looked at me with wide eyes and shock that I might lie to a customs officer.

"Well, he took me by surprise, and I didn't want to seal my pistol until we reached Alaska. What if we needed it?" I was not sure my response sounded any good to me, much less to John. Then I remembered the fishing license. "I assume you are planning to fish the first chance we get, why didn't you buy a license?" I wanted to shift the focus away from my discomfort and toward John.

"After that speech about money, I did not want to spend any on a fishing license."

"So, no fishing along the way?"

"Well, I'll see how it looks, but you took a chance back there."

By this point we only covered forty-two miles in two hours and the gravel road offered no safe way to make up time. We drove several miles without talking while I relived the customs interview in my mind. *"What was I thinking,"* I wondered, but my stomach settled the further we got from the Canadian customs officer.

We began to climb in elevation as we left the Chilkat River valley and headed west toward the headwaters of the Klehini River. The sun shone brightly on the river shimmering off the ripples in the water. The road ran along the milky white glacier water of the river and the tall pine trees became fewer and farther apart. Soon we found ourselves above timberline and crossed Chilkat Pass, elevation 3,493 feet above sea level, the highest point on the Haines Highway. The pass gave us a broad landscape view of the miles ahead.

# The Yukon

Soon we began a descent from timberline and into more of a wooded area and passed the border between British Columbia and the Yukon. We stopped to take pictures of each of us on the large wooden sign welcoming us to the Yukon.

Before leaving Texas, even though I never smoked, I thought I should start smoking a pipe, just to look cool as we journeyed the wilderness of the northwest. As John got ready to take my picture, I remembered the pipe and asked him to wait. I jumped down, ran to the car, and retrieved it. Settling again on the Yukon sign I tried my best to look like an intrepid explorer with my pipe jutting out of the side of my mouth. Turned out I did not like the pipe and the hassle of trying to load it, light it, and then smoke it. Mostly, I did not like smoking, so that fad and my effort of looking cool, became short lived.

In an attempt to bolster my outdoorsman appearance, I also began growing a beard. I hoped a few weeks would produce a full, dark beard to fill out my narrow face, but it never happened. After six weeks without shaving, I had a good mustache and goatee, but little on my cheeks and jawline. The result led to my shaving around the mustache and goatee from mid-August forward.

Looking back on the experience, I learned two things. I did not like smoking and my genes did not support a full beard.

The Yukon provided broad valleys, green forests, lots of undergrowth about four feet high, and open landscapes. We saw very few buildings or structures of any kind, but lots of icy, snow-capped mountain peaks, mostly to the west. Soon we passed places we could not pronounce. A sign showed an old native American village, Klukshu, off to the right. The village got its name from the Klukshu band of the inland Tinglits who traded with the coastal Chilkats. A short way down a dirt road we found some deserted log cabins, the remains of a meat cache about nine feet off the ground, and the Klukshu River. By then, we knew to pronounce cache as "cash," so I repeated the word to John until he gave me a dirty look. John thought the meandering stream offered a good fishing spot but the delays of the morning and the slow going on the gravel road convinced us to get back on the road to Haines Junction.

A few miles past Klukshu we passed a wide lake with another name we could not pronounce. The road paralleled Lake Dezadeash for about nine miles. The lake was long but shallow, and we saw no one; not a boat, ramp, or canoe for the entire length of the lake. Our Milepost book claimed the lake was a stopover on the old Dalton Trail from Dawson Creek to the Alaska coast, used primarily during the Klondike gold rush as an alternative to the steep climb out of Skagway into the Yukon. That day no one used the lake and we joined only a few travelers along the road beside it.

Dalton Peak stood watch over the lake from the west and looked much higher than its recorded elevation of 6,461 feet above sea level, well above timberline. Its dramatic appearance in height came partly because the elevation of the lake was 2,100 feet, and partly because its snow-covered top reminded us of much higher mountains. The snow-capped peak looked rugged and exceptionally high to us despite its modest elevation. We pushed north to Haines Junction.

Reaching Haines Junction, a major stopping point on the Alcan Highway, led us to understand dots on the map and descriptions in the Milepost for this neck of the woods involved hyperbole and exaggeration. What the book called a major stopping point was little more than a small collection of buildings. It had a garage, one store for canned goods and staples that the Milepost book misleadingly described as a shopping center, a motel, and a gas station. Gasoline came in one variety and sold for fourteen cents per liter or a little over fifty cents a gallon. We gulped, but paid the asking price, almost double the cost of a gallon of gasoline in Texas. We had no choice. Another gas station was not likely for another one hundred miles, so we filled up.

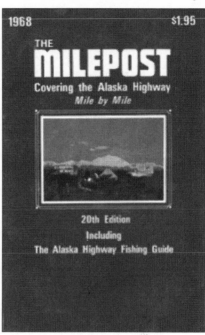

Milepost Guide,
1968 edition

From Haines Junction we turned northwest, and the topography changed. We no longer had snow-capped peaks on both sides of the road. Now the towering peaks lay to the left or west side of the road. A broad plateau lay to the east toward Whitehorse, capital of the Yukon. The boreal forest thinned in this area, but the undergrowth remained thick. It revealed no trails and looked almost impenetrable, discouraging any side hikes into the wilderness.

The late afternoon arrived, and we began looking for a place to sleep for the night. Tok, Alaska lay three hundred miles and another six hours away. Though disappointed at not making better time, we decided to stop and rest for the night. No motel or cabin for us, we planned to rough it in the Yukon. Both of us were excited to be so far from home and much closer to Alaska than the week before.

To lessen our hunger before stopping for the night, we broke out some Vienna Wieners, two kinds of mustard, and some crackers. We had some cokes to wash down the mixture and laughed that we only had forty-eight cans of wieners left. We made a mock toast to Truman Doss, our benefactor for the wieners.

For the next twenty miles we drove the gentle incline to Boutillier Summit, the highest point between Whitehorse and Fairbanks, at 3,200 feet elevation. Most all of the drive included elevations above timberline. The bare surfaces showed multiple colors: brown, yellow, ochre, and streaks of red and white. We saw no fields or cultivation for as far as our eyes could see. From the summit we could see a huge lake, Lake Kluhane, to the northwest. The surface glistened from the sun's reflection and varied from deep blue to green to a hazel color for contrast. The lake covered the land next to the road for another thirty-five miles.

At Slim's River Bridge we crossed an ancient terminal glacier moraine at the head of Lake Kluhane. The river ran down from the southwest, but we could not see any remnants of the glacier. It receded ten miles or so up river. We could see the icy snow-capped peaks of Mount Bartlett and Bighorn Peak to the west, both well above timberline. As soon as we passed the river, we saw high bluffs to our left with a herd of several dozen Dall sheep dotting the landscape. The sight of the bright, white coats of wool on the sheep excited us. As two Texas boys, we had never seen such animals. We slowed down an watched the sheep for a couple of miles.

Close to 8 p.m. we decided to camp soon even though more daylight remained. We drove to Destruction Bay along Lake Kluhane and began looking for a spot. The bay received its name during the gold-rush days because a number of boats wrecked with lives lost during storms on the lake. We saw no boats on the lake that day. We passed a small lodge and café but did not stop there. Instead we traveled a few miles more and stopped near a creek feeding into the lake.

We pulled off the road a short distance and got out to stretch. We decided this spot was sufficiently away from the road and provided a good camping spot. Without thinking of the fishing license, John pulled out his trusty fishing rod and tried his luck in the creek while I set up a makeshift camp. I laid out our sleeping bags, arranged our gear, and built a small fire. When John returned with no fish, we heated some beef stew for dinner. We drank the ice-cold water of the stream feeding into the lake. We felt like pioneers or gold-rush participants far into the Yukon Territory of Canada.

## Mosquitoes

The air was cool, but not too cold and the twilight lingered well past 11 p.m. We bedded down in our sleeping bags to rest for the final push the next day, hopefully all the way to Anchorage. Soon we realized our mistake.

Huge, we are talking sparrow sized, mosquitoes swarmed all over our faces, the only part of our bodies outside the sleeping bags. I slapped a couple and tried to get my arm right back into the bag as quickly as possible. One smashed against my palm. It measured at least a quarter inch in size, or at least it appeared that way to me. We both tried to scrunch down into the sleeping bags to minimize our exposure, but it proved futile.

After 15 minutes of stinging mosquito bites all over my face I announced the car would be my next sleeping spot. John immediately joined me. We struggled out of our sleeping bags and headed for the car. He took the front seat and I nestled into the back. We laughed about how the wilderness may look good to the eye, but it could be damaging to the body. We marveled at the size of the mosquitoes.

We talked about how we did not notice the size of the mosquitoes earlier and chalked it up to our moving around and the busy-ness of fishing and fixing something to eat. John remarked he felt a few mosquitoes while he fished, but we agreed they must have waited for us to settle in before launching the full out attack. Both of us agreed we had never seen mosquitoes as large and as voracious as those living in the Yukon.

After our discussion of the mosquitoes and plans for reaching Anchorage the next day, we settled in to sleep. Before nodding off, John asked me if I saw anyone I knew that day. We both knew the answer was "No."

The car shielded us from further mosquito attacks, and although a tad cramped, we got a reasonable amount of sleep. The bright morning light appearing by 4 a.m., and our desire to push toward the end of our journey, cut the sleeping short. A little after 4 we hurriedly threw the sleeping bags into the back seat and resumed our trek. We confirmed by looking at the map this should be our last day on the road and despite the less than greatest sleeping arrangement, we could not wait to move along.

It was Saturday, June 15, one week after we drove away from Morton, Texas.

We left the lake behind at Burwash Landing, latitude 61° 21' North, a small settlement with a motel, grocery store, and airstrip. To the west we could see Mt. Logan, elevation 19,951, towering over the mountains to the west. Mt. Lucania, the third highest peak in the St. Elias mountains, topped out at 17,150 feet and also came into view. The Milepost showed Mt. Logan was the highest elevation in Canada and second only to Mount McKinley, later called Denali, as the highest spot in North America. With the early morning light bouncing off its peak, it looked spectacular to us.

John and I both had spent time in Colorado, he fishing near Creede and I at Camp Shoshoni near the front range, and thought we knew high mountains, at least those with 14,000-foot elevations. By comparison, Mt. Logan looked amazing. Its top sneaked in and out of the clouds as we drove further and further north and provided magnificent views as we headed for Alaska. We felt like we belonged in a travelogue movie advertising the beauty of the Yukon.

Soon we passed the Donjec and White Rivers, both rushing to the northeast to join the Yukon River. Both carried prodigious volumes of water from the snow and glacial runoffs with the light colored, bluish interlaced with milky white ribbons, characteristic of such rivers. June was the month for the highest runoff and the flows we saw confirmed that fact. John commented how neither looked conducive to fishing because the water flowed so rapidly.

By mid-morning we came to Beaver Creek Canadian Customs where all vehicles stopped for inspection. We remained about twenty miles from the border, but Beaver Creek supplied the last settlement before the border. The officials gave us the once over, looked at the stamped entry permit we got back when we entered Canada, and waived us through. I relaxed when no one asked about firearms. The officer told us the time changed when we crossed into Alaska. We needed to set our clock to Alaska Standard Time, one hour back from Yukon Western Standard Time.

## Alaska Finally

He also mentioned the blacktop started at the border but to be cautious because permafrost underlying the pavement caused the road to heave and settle. He cautioned us not to speed because the permafrost created bumps and dips and no warning signs appeared along the highway. An unfamiliar word, permafrost, tempered our excitement about seeing blacktop again. The unfamiliar word confirmed we neared our destination and led us to drive slower than we planned. Sure enough, a few miles up the road we crossed the border into Alaska and welcomed an asphalt surface under our tires.

We experienced a good, level highway for several miles and our speed crept toward seventy miles per hour until we hit the predicted heaves, bumps, and dips. The Pontiac at that speed caused us to think we climbed aboard a rollercoaster ride as we rose and dipped to the uneven pavement. John kept us on the road despite a couple of scary moments, and backed off to a more reasonable fifty mph. We looked at each other and remarked how the border officer meant what he told us.

At Tetlin Junction we passed the junction of the Alaska Highway and the Taylor Highway. The Taylor Highway turns north to Eagle, a small former steamship port along the Yukon River and the historic placer-gold claims of the 1890's. In 1968, few of the gold claims produced any gold, but a few still remained active. The junction had a lodge, café, gas station, and souvenir shop with local handicrafts from the Tetlin Reserve Indians. It was the biggest collection of buildings we had seen since Juneau. One of the main attractions was the Shleekai, native language for "little dogs," Kennels, home to American Kennel Club registered Siberian husky dogs. The strong, muscular dogs were most famous for their blue eyes. We slowed but did not stop.

Right outside Tetlin, we crossed the Tanana River flowing north another two hundred miles to Fairbanks. The river flowed heavy and carried the now familiar milky-white color of the other glacier fed rivers of the region. Our excitement built as we closed in on Tok, where, in another twelve miles or so, we would leave the Alaskan Highway and turn southwest for Anchorage.

After feeling a little more out of the wilderness at Tetlin Junction and its buildings, Tok gave even more evidence we had returned to civilization. Another custom office required us to stop, but waived us through quickly when the officer saw our paperwork from earlier. The settlement had a Post Office, a modern clinic with a resident physician, a tourist information office, several stores, modern motels, service stations, a school, an Alaska State Trooper post, highway maintenance depot, and churches. We thought it a veritable city compared to the recent places we visited.

Tok lay at 63° 20' North latitude and 1,620 feet in elevation. As the summer unfolded, this marked the point farthest north of all our travels. Anchorage was southwest and mostly at sea level, so our remaining journey would drop south on the globe and go lower in elevation.

The town lay in a broad, open expanse of land. We could see the Alaska Mountain Range with its towering Mt. McKinley far to the west, but clouds covered the tops of the mountains. Nevertheless, the mountains looked huge from our vantage point. We could also see the Chugach Mountains to the south. Both ranges had lots of snow and ice at the higher elevations and added a cake-like white icing look to the vistas from Tok.

It was late morning, and not wanting to break out the Vienna Wieners, we stopped for a bite to eat and check the map for the rest of the journey to Anchorage. Our early departure put us in Tok well before lunchtime, but we were hungry. We feasted on sourdough pancakes, bacon, and hot coffee. It sure beat the warmed-up beef stew, cokes, and potato chips we ate the last few days and tasted decidedly better than wieners.

The map showed the Glenn Highway, Alaska #1, turning south from the Alaskan Highway that proceeded on toward Fairbanks. We knew this was the last leg of our journey and were almost giddy about completing our trek. Only 328 miles and six hours lay between us and our destination. Barring any disastrous delays, we would reach Anchorage before dark.

# Chapter 7
# Anchorage or Bust

We turned south onto the Glenn Highway, Alaska #1, toward Anchorage. Our final destination was within reach, and we felt a huge relief that our days on the road would soon end. The countryside did not change much, still plenty of wide-open spaces with the distant mountains in the background. The paved road was good but still had the occasional warning sign about permafrost heaves and dips. I took my turn driving at Tok and kept close to sixty mph as we headed out. We felt good after the breakfast and stretching our legs. Six more hours in the car felt like a kid's game after the week we spent in the Pontiac and on the ferry.

After thirty-five miles or so we passed some lakes and road signs warning us of bears. To this point the Dall sheep were the only wildlife along the way and we relished the hope of seeing a bear. It was not to be. The landscape turned scrubby with few tall trees and rolling valleys until we passed the Bartel Creek at mile marker forty-one. This marked the divide between the Tanana River, a tributary of the Yukon River system flowing north and west into the Bering Sea and the Copper River system emptying into the North Pacific near Cordova on the Gulf of Alaska. The divide was more like rolling over a hill. We topped out at a 2,450 feet, just below timberline. Only brush and skinny pine trees less than 10 feet tall covered the summit.

We traveled another forty miles down the valley to where the Gulkana River meets the Copper River. To the southeast we had splendid views of Mt. Drum, 12,000 feet, and Mt. Sanford, 16,200 feet, both covered with snow and ice.

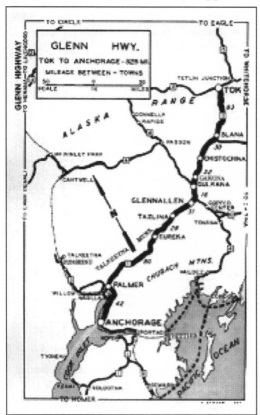

Glenn Highway courtesy of
Milepost Guidepost 1968 edition

Another few miles down the road we passed Glennallen where the road split. Highway #1 took a sharp right headed west and Highway 4 continued south to Valdez. The U.S. Army completed this section of the highway during WW II and named it for Captain E.F. Glenn who commanded expeditions through this part of Alaska in 1898 and 1899. Lt. Henry Allen, also with the U.S. Army, explored the Copper and Tanana Rivers in 1885. He and Captain Glenn lent their names to the small village of Glennallen. We turned west toward Anchorage.

The highway in this area cuts across the southern rim of a

vast tableland which reaches from the south slopes of the Alaska range, eighty miles to the north, and the Chugach Range only fifteen miles to the south. Tall trees were scarce, but willows, birches, and northern shrubs grew everywhere. The Milepost noted these as plentiful food for moose. We saw moose crossing signs along the highway but saw no moose. The depression which lay between the highway and the Chugach range extended for close to 150 miles east to west with the Matanuska River valley ending at the Knik arm of Cook Inlet, only fifty miles from Anchorage. Our excitement built as we saw map locations closer and closer to Anchorage.

## Matanuska Glacier

The highway climbed slowly for the next sixty miles from the 1,400-foot elevation at Glennallen to Tahneta Pass, the high-

Matanuska Glacier, Alaska
Photo courtesy of The Milepost, 1968 edition

est point on the Glenn Highway at 3,327 feet above sea level. At this point the upper limits of timberline with few trees gave unobstructed views south toward the Chugach range. We could see several glaciers coming down from the ice and snowbound peaks across the mountains. A few miles further along we used a turnout spot to view the Matanuska Glacier. A week before we did not know the word, but after boarding its eponym, the ferry boat, MV Matanuska, in Prince Rupert, we now understood the name tied back to this famous Alaskan Glacier. The river of ice stood about a quarter mile south of the highway and snaked its way up into the mountain tops.

The valley glacier, existing in a valley floor, as opposed to an alpine glacier hanging from mountain slopes, covered an area twenty-seven miles long by four miles wide. As an active glacier it moved about one foot per day in the summer months with the guidebook showing snow falling up-glacier taking 250 years to reach its terminus. It was the largest glacier accessible by car and enjoyed the status of one of Alaska's main tourist attractions.

The glacier also created a natural phenomenon known as a "weather hole." This occurs when chilly air of the glacier propels the warm valley air skyward resulting in sunny skies and a microclimate of mild weather around the glacier. We noticed the open sky and moderate temperature while looking across at the glacier.

An information sign at the turn off mentioned the blue ice visible in the glacier. The density of the glacier ice, due to its tremendous weight, allows the absorption of the entire spectrum of light with the exception of blue light, which the ice reflects. Our eyes noted blue sections and streaks across the ice wall at the end of the glacier. This was our first view of a glacier from a close distance. The Mendenhall Glacier outside Juneau we viewed from the ferry, but this one lay close to the highway.

We followed the Matanuska River down the valley toward Palmer. The 1960 census listed 1,183 people living in the main town in the Matanuska valley. The valley was known as the location of a government-subsidized colony of settlers in 1935 to set up farms and homes. When we came through, less than thirty-five years later, the valley was home to dairy herds, poultry, and livestock. The valley with its fertile soil and its long days of sunlight during the summer provided excellent conditions for garden and grain crops. Some of its vegetables reached world-record sizes. We sensed a return to civilization because Palmer had grocery and liquor stores, a garage and auto service, motels, cafes, churches, schools, and a variety store.

Just south of Palmer we crossed the Knik River with its silty water and glacial runoff. This area often experienced a flash flood caused by the self-dumping of Lake George several miles away at the outlet of the Knik Glacier. The year before it received a National Natural Landmark designation for its propensity to create a large glacier-dammed lake that then emptied annually for the fifty previous years. The glacier blocked the lake outlet and the lake swelled with water until summer brought warmer temperatures and the ice dam broke. The result allowed vast amounts of water to break free in a spectacular and tumultuous torrent into the Knik River. We learned the settlers held an annual contest to guess the date and time of the ice dam collapse and flood. In 1967 the flood did not occur, and some scientists thought the 1964 earthquake may have shifted the landscape making its recurrence less likely each year. We hoped to get across the river before experiencing a flash flood, and we did. Crossing the Knik River put us less than thirty miles from Anchorage.

We passed a tiny community called Eagle River. It, too, looked like civilization with its motels, laundromat, post office, and bank. Several small houses dotted the area east of the highway. A small river meandered west to join the Knik Arm of Cook

Inlet. We knew only a few miles remained and we began talking about what to do when we arrived in Anchorage.

## Reaching Anchorage

Right outside the city we passed Elmendorf Air Force Base, set up in 1940 as Elmendorf Field. The Army Air Corps, predecessor organization of the U.S. Air Force developed the air field. Soon after it became functional, personnel and materials poured in to support the area against the threat from Japanese forces during World War II. In early 1942, the U.S. formed the Eleventh Air Force wing at Elmendorf and the field played a vital role as the main coordination center and staging area during the Aleutian Campaign and later air operations against the Kuril Islands of Japan. These islands remain disputed territory today, both Japan and Russia claiming sovereignty over them.

After World War II, due to its proximity to the USSR, the field played a crucial role in early detection and response from Soviet aircraft during the cold war. As the northernmost base within the Air Force, Elmendorf was an essential part in the strategic defense of the lower forty-eight states.

Passing the base entrance we saw the Anchorage, Alaska city limits sign. We laughed and cheered as our eight-day, 7,500-mile journey was about to end. After a few moments of celebration, John turned to me and asked, "Now, what?" I did not have a ready answer, but we enjoyed the moment and felt good about our trek to Alaska.

In 1968 Anchorage was home to about 135,000 people including military personnel, making it by far the largest population center in the state. The city of Anchorage sits on a strip of flat coastal lowland which extends up the lower alpine slopes of the

Chugach Mountains making its location one of remarkable beauty. The mountains and dense forests of spruce, birch and aspen add to the contrast from the waters of Cook Inlet. The city offers magnificent marine and mountain panoramas from several spots within its boundaries.

Our view of the mountains was clear from Palmer into the city. The city extends out into the Cook Inlet near its northern end where it splits into two arms. We came in from the north and east across the Knik Arm. The colorful name, Turnagain Arm, identified the southern arm of the Cook Inlet. It received its name from the famous, or infamous, Captain William Bligh of the HMS Bounty fame. Bligh served as Captain Cook's Sailing Master on his third and final voyage seeking a Northwest Passage from the Pacific Ocean to the Atlantic. In 1778 when they reached the head of Cook Inlet Bligh thought both Knik and Turnagain Arms were mouths of rivers, but hoped they might lead to an opening for the Northwest Passage. Cook ordered Bligh to organize a party to travel up Knik Arm, which returned quickly reporting the river only a few miles away. Later a second party went up Turnagain Arm only to return reporting only a river lay ahead. Frustrated in the results of the second party that had to 'turn again' and return, the southern arm received the name. Early maps from the expedition label Turnagain Arm as Turnagain River.

The fjord extends in an east-west direction for forty plus miles and forms part of the northern boundary of the Kenai Peninsula and reaches to within twelve miles of Portage Bay on the western end of Prince William Sound in the northern Pacific. Turnagain Arm witnesses some of the world's highest tides, beginning with a tidal bore on especially large tides. The flood tides can reach six feet high and travel six mph. Turnagain Arm became a well-attended tourist area welcoming fishermen, hunters, wildlife photographers, and weekend visitors. Easily accessible from Anchorage many head for the scenic waters to watch beluga whales swimming in the fjord.

Our guidebook cautioned us against walking on the treacherous mudflats that appeared at low tide in Turnagain Arm. When the water recedes the glacial silt often becomes like quicksand. We read of unwary victims walking onto the seemingly solid silt only to find themselves caught in the mud.

Anchorage also serves as the transportation hub for the state with two of the three main roads and the Alaska Railroad passing through town. It began as the construction headquarters and survey camp for building the Alaska Railroad in 1914, saw tremendous growth after World War II, and saw another growth spurt after Alaska became a state in 1959. Its mild climate compared to other parts of the state, made it attractive for settlers and business development. In winter months the temperature averaged thirteen degrees Fahrenheit and fifty-seven degrees during July with fifteen inches of precipitation during the year and only light winter snowfall.

Anchorage's location at 61° North latitude and 149.9° West longitude, gives it a unique location on the globe for air travel. Its international airport served as "Air Crossroads of the North." Transpolar flights from Europe—it sits 4,488 miles and about nine hours from London—regularly stop for refueling in route to cities in Asia. Anchorage lies 3,370 miles from New York City, 3,464 miles from Tokyo, and 4,362 miles from Moscow.

We drove into downtown Anchorage to look for a phone booth to call our contact and announce our arrival. Remnants of the great earthquake of 1964 greeted us. Even though the downtown area lay seventy-five miles northwest of the epicenter, it suffered heavy damage. Parts of the city built on sandy bluffs overlooking Cook Inlet suffered landslide damage. We drove in along Fifth Street, ventured west until we reached an end at L

Street. There we turned right and then right again on Fourth Street, one of the main arteries of downtown Anchorage. The sights stunned us. We saw the street split by a subsidence of the north side of the street, leaving the south side about eight feet higher. We traveled the repaired road, but saw the damaged buildings and the dramatic difference between the road then and where it was before the earthquake.

The great Alaskan Earthquake, sometimes referred to as the Good Friday Earthquake, occurred on Friday afternoon, March 27, 1964, at 5:36 p.m. along a fault between the Pacific and North American plates in Prince William Sound in the Northern Pacific Ocean. The focus of the quake lay on the ocean floor fifteen miles below the earth's surface. The quake lasted over four minutes becoming one of the most powerful earthquakes recorded in North American history, reaching a magnitude of 9.2. Six hundred miles of fault ruptured at once and moved up to sixty feet, releasing hundreds, if not thousands of years' built-up stress. Officials reported the subduction zone earthquake resulted when an oceanic plate slid under the continental plate. The quake occurred along a fault identified as the Aleutian Megathrust and caused much of the uneven ground shifts, sometimes hundreds of miles away from the epicenter. Some parts of Alaska reported vertical displacements up to thirty-eight feet. In all, the quake affected an area of over 100,000 square miles of the state. We saw some of it first-hand in downtown Anchorage.

The shifts in the ocean floor created huge tsunamis up to 220 feet high, which resulted in many of the deaths and much of the property damage. Official measurements noted the tsunamis in Japan and the waves reached as far away as Peru in South America. Much of the subsidence and resulting tsunami action happened along Turnagain Arm. The upheaval and tidal action destroyed the small villages of Girdwood and Portage, thirty and forty miles southeast of Anchorage. Girdwood moved inland and

Portage became abandoned. About twenty miles of the Seward Highway sank below the high-water mark of Turnagain Arm. This necessitated repairs and raising bridges along the route from 1964 through 1966.

We saw the fifteen story Anchorage Westward Hotel tower to our left. We had read how the tallest building in Alaska and its famous hotel, received as guests, Senator John F. Kennedy in 1960, before he became president, and the Beatles and President Lyndon Johnson in 1966. The Beatles, flying from London to Tokyo encountered unfavorable weather and made an unscheduled stop. Their nine-hour stay created a local sensation when the news got out they were in town. The hotel sustained substantial damage from the earthquake, but it still towered over the rest of the downtown. Many city blocks had a jumble of repaired buildings, new construction, and rubble-strewn lots.

4th Street, Anchorage, Alaska, March 29, 1964
Anchorage Westward Hotel in background
Photo courtesy of University of Washington Archives

A large section of town slid into Cook Inlet. The resulting jumble of land and coastline became Earthquake Park, an area we visited several times in the coming months. Parts of downtown near the Alaska Railroad also slid into the inlet destroying several acres of buildings and city blocks in downtown Anchorage. Despite the passing of four years since the quake, we clearly saw the damage the quake caused.

The earthquake, occurring barely five years from Alaska receiving statehood, found Anchorage with many characteristics of a boom town. Many buildings received poor earthquake engineering, or none at all. The town's infrastructure such as streets, sidewalks, sewer mains, and water lines offered little resistance to the stress brought by the earthquake and collapsed or ruptured in several landslide zones. During the summer of 1968 we saw many rebuilding or repair projects around the area.

## Our Local Contact

Parts of the downtown area looked fine, but other parts looked like the earthquake happened only a month or so before. We looked for a place to park and phone Richard Schultz, our local contact. Our trek north ended around 4 p.m. on Saturday, June 15 when we exited the Pontiac to make the phone call. We had been on the road for seven and a half days.

We made Richard's first connection through local friends in our hometown. He was married to a sister of a local resident. John spoke to him three times over the past month, but I had only spoken to him once. Neither of us had met him. We made the call and provided our address in downtown Anchorage. Richard indicated he would come quickly and direct us to his home.

We walked around the block somewhere between 4th and 5th Streets and Gambell Street, waiting for Richard to arrive. He did not disappoint, arriving within fifteen minutes. He looked about fifty years old, had a slight widow's peak to his hairline, and a slight build. John and I both stood several inches taller. He identified himself quickly as he got out of his car. We guessed there were not too many tall Texans standing around in downtown Anchorage on Saturday afternoon. After greetings and the usual, how was the trip questions, we followed him to his home in the south part of town.

On the way John mentioned the last shower we had was on the Ferry, three days earlier. I took a quick smell check of my armpit and announced my body odor did not meet the standard for meeting polite company. John felt the same. We agreed to inquire about a shower or bath before we sat down to an extended conversation with people we had never met. It all turned out well when, Betty, Richard's wife, greeted us by saying we probably first wanted to freshen up after the long trip. We hoped she did not smell us coming when we stepped into their house.

Half an hour later, after two quick showers and a light year's difference in our general aspect and attitude, we helped Richard set up a grill in the backyard. We told him how glad we were to be there and how much we appreciated their hospitality. He responded it was nothing and he hoped everyone in Alaska would greet us warmly. Then he said something that changed the tenor of the conversation and ignited our anxiety.

## Disturbing News

Richard said, "The jobs I thought we had lined up require union membership." Suddenly, our appetites evaporated.

He explained how his contact at the lumber company indicated they always needed summer workers and could easily take on two more young workers. When Richard called earlier in the week to announce our expected arrival and availability the company asked for our union membership registration. Of course, we had no such thing. The International Woodworkers of America served as the industrial union of lumbermen, sawmill workers, and transportation workers and dominated the industry in the western states and Canada. As it turned out, many of the eastern colleges let out for summer earlier than the Texas colleges and college men from the east filled many of the summer jobs. Those men also knew a lot more about labor unions than we did. Farmers and ranchers in west Texas had no use for unions and we never imagined joining one. Now we needed such membership and we needed it fast.

Richard explained how this crucial detail somehow never came up in his discussions with the company and how embarrassed he felt telling us now. Apparently, joining the International Woodworkers of America could take from three to four weeks and required a recommendation from a member. We had neither the time nor the recommendation. Suddenly, we sorely needed a job.

My mind raced to crazy places before I said anything. The last thing I wanted to do was pile into the Pontiac and drive back to Texas. John's face reflected an "Oh, No," look similar to the one the Wiley Coyote flashed right before he vanished from the Roadrunner's latest trick in the popular cartoons.

Finally, I stammered, "What do you suggest?"

In a calm voice, surely practiced by Richard before our arrival, he relayed that other summer jobs were available, and he was following up with other contacts in town. He acted confident we could get some kind of jobs in the area, he just did not know where. Somehow that failed to dampen our anxiety.

While we picked at the hamburgers and potato salad for supper that night, not regaining our appetites after the news, we laid out a game plan for the coming week. Richard had a list of companies to contact about employment and we began plotting their addresses on the city map. We listed them in order of miles from Richard's house and made a mental commitment to start early on Monday morning. Richard pledged to make more calls beginning on Monday, but it became clear finding a job fell to us. The thrill of ending our travels disappeared when we found this new obstacle to a successful summer in Alaska.

Lucky for us, Richard arranged for us to help a friend on Sunday, so we did not have to sit around and worry all day. His friend was building a new home just south of the city and needed some general clean up and material arranging before his work crew showed up Monday morning. Richard offered us as the labor, and we gladly jumped at the chance.

Early Sunday morning we rode with Richard out to this fellow's site and took some general directions on what he needed. Mostly, we cleared debris and trash from the work site and piled lumber according to a layout he provided. It was hard, but welcome work, and he agreed to pay $2 per hour. That rate far exceeded the going wage for laborers in Texas, but we knew we could not work enough hours on that Sunday to help us overall.

While we worked Richard and his friend sat not far away among some large spruce trees. The owner had parked a small travel trailer at the edge of the lot, and they periodically went in and out for coffee. We could hear them talking about the coming week. Of course, we thought the most important thing for the coming week was to get jobs, but they were talking about the midnight sun.

Later that week, when Thursday night turned into Friday morning, Alaska would see the summer solstice, or the longest day of the year with the sun at its peak. Anchorage was an excellent location to see the effect on daily routines and the population. The sunset would arrive around 11:45 p.m. and the next morning's sunrise would come at 4:20 a.m., barely four and a half hours later. That meant over twenty hours of sunlight and given an hour and a half each for dusk and predawn light, continuous across the city.

The amount of daylight on the year's longest day depends on your location. If any part of the sun's disc is above the horizon, it counts as daylight. In Alaska, even though the entire state brags about the midnight sun, technically one's position must be above the Arctic Circle, 66° North latitude, to have no sunset at all on the summer solstice. Fairbanks and Nome, Alaska lay just below the required latitude, but do experience twenty-four hours of civil twilight.

Anchorage hosted several midnight sun activities. The citizens made an unofficial holiday of it. Seems folks stayed up all night, played softball without artificial lights, went on hikes, or climbed into the Chugach Mountain range to watch the sun set and then rise over the city. Others celebrated with farmer's markets, street fairs, and pie eating contests. All of that sounded like fun, but we only thought about how it would supply us more daylight to find a job. We pushed back on the urge to panic at our situation.

As nice as our hosts were to us, we knew we could not stay with them indefinitely. First, we needed a job, then we needed a place to stay. These factors pressed down on us more than celebrating the midnight sun. We finished our labors and wondered what Monday might bring.

# In the Land of the Midnight Sun

# Chapter 8
# Employment and Public Housing

We rose early on Monday, June 17, to a sunny day with clear skies, eager to launch our job search. The jolting news Richard delivered on Saturday about having no jobs lined up for us injected some urgency to our effort. Betty provided a hot breakfast of eggs, toast, jam, orange juice, and coffee. I was already jittery but drank a third cup of coffee while we talked. We had several potential employers on our list and a map of the city to guide us. We felt as prepared as two out-of-state tenderfeet could with less than forty-eight hours as visitors to Anchorage under our belts. Richard told us he would resume calling after 9 a.m.

First stop at a Sears store supplied little hope. A tough looking lady in coveralls stood behind the help desk and greeted us with a nod, but no conversation. After telling her we wanted jobs, she handed us a two-page information sheet to fill out. Of course we used Richard's address and phone number for our local contact information. When she said all applications first went to Chicago and the home office, we turned around and walked out.

Mid-morning we stopped at a lumber yard on the Seward Highway south of downtown. The yard manager told us to go into the main building and ask for Rod. Inside another tough

113

looking lady greeted us and said Rod was busy, but if we waited in the nail, screw, and studs section he should be available shortly. The lady offered us coffee while we waited, but we declined, feeling caffeinated enough for the day. After ten minutes or so, Rod appeared and welcomed us into his small office with a window looking out into the nail, screw, and studs section of the store. We declined his offer of coffee and said the lady offered us the same. We quickly told him our plight. He seemed impressed or bewildered, we drove from Texas without having a job nailed down.

"We need some help, but I did not know people were coming from Texas for our jobs." His opening statement sounded encouraging, until he followed it with, "Can you drive a forklift?"

I thought, *"How hard can it be?"* John looked at me as though he did not want to repeat the scene with the customs officer at the border out of Haines when I lied about having a firearm. He said nothing but I sensed from his look he wanted to play this straight. Rod could ask us to mount a forklift to demonstrate our skills, quickly removing all doubt about our experience or skill with such equipment. We conceded we had no such experience.

Rod continued the discussion for another few minutes before welcoming us to Alaska and wishing us well in our search. He mentioned a construction company down the road might be hiring but followed that with, "Do you belong to a union?" We felt crushed and despondent as we drove to the next company on the list.

After talking with three more companies before mid-afternoon we learned Rod was an exception. Most folks hardly gave us the time of day, much less spent fifteen minutes talking with us. He at least was courteous and showed some interest in us as people even though he did not have a job for us. We found others dismissive of us completely. Growing up used to southern hospitality, we figured they must be really busy.

By 5 p.m. and no viable prospects, we decided to return to Richard and Betty's to see if any leads popped up on their end. No, we discovered. We ate supper and prepared for bed feeling low. We compared notes and cash on us and figured we could stay two weeks at the most without a real job. Of course, we hoped Richard had other friends who might employ us at $2 per hour doing odd jobs and manual labor. On Sunday we each earned $12 but knew that would not go far if we had to pay rent, buy food, and gas, and have a little spending money to see the area. Tuesday presented another day and Anchorage was indeed a beautiful place. We just wondered how long we could stay.

We both had experience with jobs. John and I had worked on farms and ranches at home in the summers. Both of us worked in retail environments, John at his family store and me at Rose Auto & Appliance, so we could offer some experience to retail employers. I worked for a while at a shop selling and installing tires on autos and trucks, so I suggested we talk to auto centers and garages. Neither of us were handy with auto repairs, but we could handle tires and accessories. As we talked, we gained a bit of optimism. Surely, someone in Alaska needed two workers.

## Continued Job Search

On Tuesday we contacted a fellow Richard called. He was an accountant and was nice enough to give us a few minutes of his time, but he wanted a bookkeeper, not two college guys with no accounting experience. We also talked with Matanuska Maid Dairy, another contact of Richards's. It was a dairy products company that collected and delivered milk and ice cream in the greater Anchorage area. Unfortunately, that lead went nowhere.

They wanted someone with a Commercial Driver's license which neither of us had. By early afternoon, our hopes sank as we received perfunctory treatment at Post Road Services, a one-stop service and supply business for trailers and campers. They turned us away without so much as a "Welcome to Alaska."

By supper time and our returning to Betty and Richard's place our spirits dragged bottom. Richard tried a pep talk about being only two days into our search and how something would surely turn up. It had negligible effect on us. That night before bed, we discussed hotels, motels, and restaurants. They needed willing, but unskilled workers to clean rooms, wash dishes, or carry out maintenance. We resolved to accept most any kind of job so long as it paid us enough to stay around. No job at this point would look menial to us.

Wednesday found us repeating our efforts of Monday and Tuesday with the same results. We talked to three motels, two restaurants, and a store that sold ranges, refrigerators, and furnaces. Following the earlier pattern, some people were nice and others not so much. Around 5 p.m. a hint of panic flashed through my mind, *"What if we have to go home?"*

That night Richard and Betty went to dinner at some friends, so we ate at a local casual café. We ate grilled cheese sandwiches with only water to drink because we wanted to make our cash reserves stretch as far as possible. John said he would take a dishwashing job at the café, but the manager said they had no openings. After telling us they had no jobs, he walked away.

We were in no hurry to return since Richard and Betty were not at home, so we just sat at the café for a while. The young waitress came over a couple of times to ask if she could bring us anything, but each time we declined her offer. The third time she came over to our table the café had a bit of a lull and she asked us where we were from. She told us she would be a senior in high school the coming fall and we figured our southern accents piqued her curiosity and caused her to engage us in conversation. We recounted our week-long drive and ferry ride from Texas to Alaska and she expressed surprise we made it in one week. She also kidded us about Texas becoming the second largest state when Alaska became a state. We took it good naturedly and told her we had to change the words to the state song from "largest and grandest" to "second-largest and grandest." She found that hilarious. We also used the time to ask her about any jobs in town. She said she did not know of any and told us she got this job because her uncle was the manager. When a couple entered the café, she left us to get them seated.

## A Tip About a Job

We paid the bill and stood up to leave when the manager came over again. He asked if we really drove to Alaska from Texas and motioned for us to sit down again. Having nothing pressing, we sat down at the same table. He took a chair at the table and asked about our trip to Anchorage. He agreed the Inside Passage route was an appropriate choice and told us about driving to Edmonton, Alberta, Canada once to pick up some commercial kitchen equipment. His experience on the Alaskan Highway proved long and tedious hauling the equipment back to Anchorage. He also asked about the ferry ride. We told him about the eagles and sleeping a lot.

After a few minutes, he stood up as if to leave. Then he turned and mentioned his wife worked as a school teacher for the Greater Anchorage Area Borough School District. We wondered what that had to do with anything when he said they might be hiring people for work cleaning and painting the school buildings during the summer break. He confirmed his niece told him we needed jobs, or we faced returning to Texas. He went to the back and returned with the address for the administrative office for the school district. We both felt as good as if he offered us an ice cream sundae on the house. We told him we would check with the school district early the next morning and thanked him for the suggestion.

We returned to our guest quarters with a glimmer of hope.

Thursday morning we announced our new lead and Richard told us how to drive over to the school district's office. Betty again provided a hearty breakfast. Richard reported his calling on Wednesday brought no new leads.

We arrived at the school district office before 9 a.m. and found no one around. We found the front door locked and no signs showing hours of operation. We returned to the car to assess our next move. Lacking any other leads, we waited.

A few minutes before 10 a.m. a lady parked next to us and looked us over. We stared back. At least someone appeared to work at the office. She locked her car, walked to the door, and unlocked it. We went right behind her.

We quickly told her someone told us they might be looking for summer workers to clean school buildings. She walked into the office, put down her purse on a desk, and put her keys in a drawer before turning to address us. "You need to go to maintenance. Their office is a block away behind ours."

We thanked her and returned to the car. Two minutes later we arrived at a large, temporary looking tin and steel building that looked like a combined bus garage and storage warehouse. We saw a couple of cars parked in front, but no one was in sight. We wandered in through the large overhead garage door someone rolled up into the open position and looked around. Still no one.

We stood for a minute or so just looking before a man came out from the rear of the storage area and waived at us to follow him. He directed us to a small office at the back of the garage. We quickly told him we sought jobs for the summer.

"You need to talk with Jim. He's on break right now, but will be available in a few minutes if you want to wait." At least he did not tell us to get lost, so we waited while wondering why someone took a break mid-morning.

Jim returned and conducted perhaps the shortest job interview in the history of job interviews. He asked if we had transportation. We did. He asked when we could be available. We told him immediately. Then he told us we needed to fill out some paperwork and could start the next morning at one of the junior high schools. John and I made up our minds when he said the job paid $2.42 per hour, which seemed like a fortune to us. We forgot to ask about the duties of the job. We practically grabbed the employment applications from his hands as we started completing them. Grins covered our faces from ear to ear as we put down name, address, and social security numbers.

When we returned the paperwork, he mentioned the school district would withhold federal income taxes, FICA deductions, and Alaska income tax from our paychecks. That last withholding came as a surprise because Texas did not have an income tax and most summer jobs at home did not bother with federal income tax withholding or paying FICA. At that point we did not care. We had JOBS!

Jim gave us an address for the school and told us to report at 8 a.m. to the crew boss, a lady named Gabriele. It dawned on us we might ask what tasks the jobs entailed. Jim's response offered no clarification. "Anything Gabriele tells you to do."

Our spirits soared as if we ascended Mt. McKinley. Whatever Gabriele asked us to do, we felt confident we could do it or bust our butts trying. Getting a paycheck would allow us to stay, live out our dream summer, and get a permanent place to sleep.

We returned to see Richard and Betty around lunch time. Betty fixed sandwiches and iced tea while we told about our jobs. It turned out at that point, we did not know much except that we could make over $90 dollars a week. They both seemed pleased, probably because it meant their guests would soon vacate the spare bedroom.

We asked for some recommendations for renting an apartment. Neither of us had much experience with that task, especially in such a faraway land. They had some ideas and gave us some phone numbers of rentals. We spent the rest of the afternoon with the air slowly leaving our excitement balloons. Apartments cost money. Some of them we found, lots of money.

Several apartments quoted $250 to $300 per month for a two-bedroom one bath arrangement. To a couple of small-town people like us, that seemed pretty high. We decided we did not need a fancy place, just a place to sleep and fix some meals, so we lowered our sights on what might be acceptable. If we could find something for half those prices, we knew we could tolerate most anything for the next two to two and a half months. The afternoon flew by and we had no good prospects for a place to live.

Richard volunteered he knew some folks in the low-income housing department for the state of Alaska and would make some calls on Friday. We thanked him and resolved to resume our search over the weekend. First, we had jobs awaiting our arrivals.

Friday morning we arrived at the junior high school address given us around 7:30 a.m. and found no one there. We double checked to confirm the address and hoped someone who soon appear. Slightly before 8 a.m. two men arrived in a pickup truck. They looked a bit rough to us, but we could not identify any particular reason for our thinking, just that they did not look like folks ready for an office job. Both men wore baseball caps with loose hair sticking out the sides and back, T-shirts, jeans, and sneakers. They lingered at the door to the school and drank from the thermos bottles they carried. John and I both wore work boots thinking we might need them for whatever tasks Gabriele assigned us, but we had no thermos.

## Janitors for the Summer

We got out and walked over to the men asking if they knew a lady named Gabriele. They said she would be there soon and told us they worked on her crew. We explained our situation and they welcomed us to the team. They told us few people arrived at work early, most everyone showed up on time or a few minutes late. Two other cars drove up exactly at 8 a.m.

A tall, blondish, fifty something year-old lady got out of the first car and walked toward us. Her general appearance was one of wholesome good looks, but when you looked closely you noticed some wrinkles to her face that suggested some travels down rough roads. One of the men informed her we were there to join the team. She turned toward us and said, "I am Gabriele. I got a call last night about you."

She turned and unlocked the doors to the school and walked in. All of us followed her. The other men walked down a hallway as if they knew their destination while John and I held back awaiting instructions. "Come with me," Gabriele said as she turned and walked toward an office. We followed her closely.

We spent the next few minutes introducing ourselves and she seemed pleased we found the school without anything more than the address. We told her how glad we were to get the jobs and were ready to follow her direction. She mentioned how one of the most important things to her was to show up sober and on time and not miss any work days. She made a casual remark about if we did that, we would be fine. She gave direct instructions but had a friendly manner.

She asked if we had experience painting, running a buffer, or operating an industrial vacuum cleaner. We answered affirmative to the painting and negative to the other two. She said we would catch on as the days passed. That day, she assigned us to cleaning class rooms, explaining we needed to dust everything, wipe down all the desks and chairs with cleaning rags soaked in a disinfectant, empty the trash cans, and then stack all the desks and chairs on one side of the room. Once we accomplished that we should move to the next room and repeat the process. Someone would follow us with wax for the half of the floor left open and then run the buffer over it. Once they completed the waxing and buffing, we would return to move the desks and chairs to the other side of the room allowing the waxing and buffing to occur on the newly opened floor. Seemed simple enough to us. We went to work on the first room with some good old-fashioned Texas enthusiasm.

By 10 a.m. we had finished three rooms when Joe, one of the men we first met, stuck his head in the door of our room and told us it was break time. We followed him to a large room that obviously served as the lunchroom during school days. Everyone gathered around and Gabriele took the opportunity to introduce us to the other workers. Many asked questions about Texas and why we came to Alaska. The fifteen minutes flew by with us doing most of the talking. We learned very little about our co-workers before heading to another classroom.

About noon Joe again stuck his head into our classroom, now on our sixth, and looked around before announcing the lunch break. He asked how many rooms we cleaned that morning and upon hearing the answer, told us we needed to slow down. We worked faster than the others and he said he knew we were new to the job, but there was no reason to break any speed records for getting the job done. He did not come right out and say it, but we took from the conversation Gabriele might be happy with our speedy work, but the other workers might resent it. Lunch break sounded good, but we brought nothing to eat or drink.

John went to the car and brought back four cans of Vienna Wieners and the brown mustard. That surprised the other workers. They did not know such little sausages existed and gave us some questioning looks as we chowed down. We drank from the water fountain in the lunchroom to wash down the little sausages. The other workers broke out sandwiches

Charlie on break, Anchorage, Alaska

and drank from thermos bottles or big water jars. Gabriele told us we should pack a lunch the following week because the break was only a half hour, and we did not have time to go pick up something. Someone mentioned the longest day of the year and how they stayed up until past midnight to see how dark it became overnight. Others made similar comments with most heading for some type of midnight sun activity over the weekend. Mostly, we answered more questions about our trip to Anchorage and the ferry ride up the Inside Passage. It surprised us none of the co-workers had been to Juneau or along the Inside Passage. From our recent experience with the ferry we got lots of questions and felt like mini celebrities.

Joe sat down next to us to explain the half hour break allowed us to leave at 4:30 p.m. and still get in an eight-hour workday. It made sense to us. 8 to noon and then 12:30 to 4:30 added up to the eight hours. We figured no one counted the morning break, or as we soon learned, the afternoon break which came at 2:30. It began to dawn on us the workday revolved around the breaks, maybe because cleaning classroom was not the most intellectually challenging thing we ever encountered. We also noticed no one hurried back to work after the breaks.

Gabriele found us around 4 p.m. as we finished our ninth classroom and asked us to gather all the trash into large bags we then took out to a dumpster. She expressed how our work so far pleased her, and she impressed upon us it was important to show up on time Monday morning. She did not mention that we might be working too fast. Her remarks led us to believe our crew might not be the most dependable workers for showing up every day and usually took their time completing tasks.

Our first day went well with the exception of our working too fast.

We told Richard and Betty all about our first day on the job and they seemed pleased. Before they could mention it, we talked about using the weekend to find a place to live. Richard had a couple of addresses for us to check out but cautioned they were for low-income people and the neighborhoods might seem a little sketchy to us. Richard mentioned that he knew we came from middle-class families and a small town. He just wanted us to know the public housing accommodations in Anchorage might not be the same standard as our homes in Morton, Texas. We told him we understood and really just wanted someplace we could afford.

## Apartment Hunting

Richard spoke the truth. The first two places we looked at were trash strewn, unkempt, dumpy looking neighborhoods. Beer cans and trash piled up around the parking spaces and the residents appeared to take aim at the dumpster at best, not bothered if their trash came close but did not make it inside the container. We adjusted our expectations as we inspected the first two places. John reminded me we DID spend the night in the Prince Rupert trash dump.

We lucked out at the third place. Most of the residents were affiliated with the military. Couples and families with a small child or two made up most of the neighbors. We found a furnished end unit with one bedroom and an efficiency style living room, kitchen, and foldout bed space combined in the main room. A bath with shower came with it. Best of all, the rent was $150 for the month. We paid for the last eight days of June and all of July. It pleased the manager we paid a month in advance, and he gave us the keys.

We returned to announce the good news to Richard and Betty who graciously said they would miss us. Richard also said, if we wanted, he lined up some work on Sunday with the same fellow as the week before. Suddenly, we felt enriched. Not only did we have a steady job, but we could also work on the weekends for more pay. Things were falling into place for us.

We moved all our stuff, which was not much, into the apartment and spent our first night there. John took the official bedroom, and I took the fold out bed in the main room. It stored easily against the wall when not used and I found it surprisingly comfortable. It sure beat sleeping in the Pontiac or on the ground. Right before we fell asleep in our new apartment, John asked if I had seen anyone we knew all week. I had not.

We had arrived in Anchorage only a week earlier and the week included some emotional difficulties, but now our outlook for an exciting summer was sunny and bright. At the time we did not know we would soon learn a lot about the earthquake, our coworkers' lives, and life's lessons learned.

# Chapter 9
# Odd Jobs & Coworkers

Sunday appeared with cloudy skies and the threat of rain. Despite the weather we felt great and looked forward to more work at $2 per hour. This time Richard did not go with us but confirmed we knew the address and how to arrive at the site. We assured him we did and could, so we set out early.

We arrived while the owner and his family ate their breakfast. They invited us to join them. We declined the meal but agreed to have a cup of coffee before we got our directions and started work. The couple's teenage daughter, fourteen, joined us. After a few giggles and smirks when the daughter listened to us talk, her mother cautioned her not to laugh at our southern accents. She tried, but she had to mention how funny we talked. At this point we came to expect some remarks about how our speaking did not sound like others in Alaska.

For that day, the man wanted us to help clear some trees and brush from his land. No trees stood on the building site itself, but several tall spruce and pine trees dotted the rest of the lot. Some of them came within thirty feet of the planned house and could pose a fire danger if a forest fire threatened the area. In addition, lots of brush and undergrowth existed just outside the cleared area. The owner wanted us to clear the land with his McCulloch chainsaw. Our eyes brightened at the prospect of working with the powerful saw. The only problem; neither of us had any experience with one.

He and the daughter went around the lot and tied ribbons to the tree trunks he wanted removed. For the brush he gave a blanket instruction to take out completely another forty feet from the edge of the clearing. He doubted if we could do it all that Sunday, but he would check on us periodically during the day. It was still cloudy and cool with a slight mist falling. Not enough to call it rain, but enough to get us into our rain jackets.

## The Chain Saw

We went to the tool shed to inspect the McCulloch gas-powered chain saw. He showed us the gasoline-oil mixture he prepared and how to fill the tank on the saw. Next, he showed us how to hold the saw, pull the cord to start it, and how to pull the trigger when we wanted to engage the saw. The roar of the motor gave us a surge of energy. I thought to myself, *"I am about to become a real, live, Alaskan woodsman."* John must have had the same idea because we both stepped forward when he asked who wanted to go first. We looked at each other but no one moved back. The landowner mentioned how there would be plenty of time manning the saw and we would need to alternate time on the saw. I did not fully understand what he meant because I saw myself cutting down trees most of the day.

Our instructions included cutting the trees first, then cutting the trunks into sizable lengths we could roll or carry to a designated pile. Most of the tree trunks ran six to eight inches in diameter so the saw would make quick work of them. However, a tree twenty feet high might then require four or five more cuts until the various lengths became manageable. With the saw idling in the background, the owner held it out and I stepped forward to take it. I would be the woodsman first and John could deal with the logs resulting from my acumen with the chain saw. I eagerly took the saw from the owner and revved it a few times just to hear the motor sounds rumble through the woods. John stood back, not smiling.

The saw weighed about seven pounds and required a two-handed grip to properly guide it through the tree trunks and then to slice off the limbs and cut the resulting logs into stackable segments. At first, I felt on top of the world quickly cutting down large trees and moving on to the limbs, but that feeling was short lived. Have you ever held your arms straight out from your body, even without lifting any weights? If so, you know what I soon learned. On the skinny side of 155 pounds my athletic prowess never came from my upper body strength. Handling the chain saw soon became a great burden. After less than five minutes, my arm muscles burned with fatigue, and I had to lower them for several seconds before I recovered sufficiently to take on another spruce tree. Not wanting John to think I was a weakling, I tried my best to continue but could not last more than a minute without another break. Luckily, the owner retreated to his trailer before my biceps screamed out for a halt.

I lasted fifteen minutes before asking John if he wanted a turn. He was busy diligently pulling the logs I cut from the tree trunks and stacking them as directed. He did not watch me that closely because he eagerly took the chain saw and stepped toward another tree. I stood back and watched hoping some feeling would soon return to my arms. John attacked the first spruce, about an eight incher, with lots of vigor. The tree fell and he attacked the limbs, cutting them away from the trunk, and then cut the trunk into six-foot segments. I continued watching while he made quick work of his first tree. John outweighed me by a few pounds and his arm muscles made me look puny, and thus far, he showed no signs of slowing down. I figured I better get working on the debris and logs while John walked to the next tree with the chain saw roaring.

As I worked on the limbs and logs, I watched John out of the corner of my eye for any signs of weariness. Sure enough, even though stronger than me, about half way through the second tree trunk, he lowered the saw and let his arms rest a bit. When he looked to see if I was watching, I quickly looked away. Soon he returned to the task, and I resumed taking quick glances his way. Like any runners in the mile run at track meets who make the first two laps too quickly, John's efforts with the saw began to slow. He lasted a little more than the fifteen minutes of my first go-around before asking if I wanted another turn with the saw.

Even though we were still in our first hour of work, I suggested a break and John agreed. We sat down on a log and drank some water, neither of us saying anything. Finally, I spoke up.

"Running that saw is a bugger."

"Yeah, it is harder than it looks." John replied.

We discussed how it turned out much less fun than we anticipated, and we still had most of the day ahead of us. We agreed to trade off duties of the saw with every tree. By then we figured taking down a tree, cutting off the limbs, and cutting the trunk into segments took about seven to ten minutes. If we switched after every tree, our arms could make it through the day. Resuming with this new plan allowed us to work until noon without taking another break.

The owner invited us to lunch on a bench-table he set up across from his trailer. His daughter prepared some pimento cheese sandwiches and lemonade for lunch and we eagerly joined them. He seemed pleased with the progress and asked us what we thought. I looked at John and then ventured a comment.

"That saw is a challenge."

"Yeah, I should have warned you. It is a challenge to keep the saw going for very long." He said what we learned by experience during the first half hour.

The light, misty rain continued. While we sat outside with our rain jackets and hats, the daughter stayed inside the little trailer. It supplied some shelter for her and the owner, but not enough room for four of us to get inside. When we finished lunch, the owner joined her inside and we returned to the trees.

We repeated our efforts of the morning and soon created a large stack of logs. We imagined our stack looked as if some real loggers built it. Of course, we had no way of knowing that, but we felt proud of our work. The limbs, on the other hand, created a huge pile where we dragged them. We found no way to make the pile look neat and tidy. We wondered how the owner might manage this excess debris. Burn it? Probably not, because of the fire danger.

By 3:30 or so the rain stopped, and the owner and his daughter came out and sat at the table as we continued to work. Soon the wind picked up signaling a change in the weather. The clouds rolled faster across the sky and the tallest trees began to sway from the wind. Because the sandstorms and winds of west Texas reached velocities much higher than this breeze, we did not think much about it and continued working. By this time we had cleared two sides of the building lot from the outline of the proposed house to the lot boundaries. We worked closer to the trailer as we moved to another side and continued the clearing work. John cut down a tree that rose ten feet or so from the trailer. The daughter watched the tree fall and seemed impressed as the tree trunk fell into the clearing.

# Earthquake Memories

As we moved to another tree and my turn with the saw, the wind began gusting more. The tall trees nearest to us swayed back and forth with the increased wind. The young girl looked up at the swaying trees and began shrieking as she fled to the trailer. Her loud cries got our attention. I feared the tree I selected was too close to the trailer and she feared it might fall on her. John and I stopped working and watched as she ran into the shelter of the trailer. The owner followed her.

We looked at the tree with a cut half way through its trunk and gauged where it would fall. It looked safe to us. John walked around the area and looked at the tree from three different sides. He announced it looked safe to him. I held the saw in the lowered position until we assessed the situation. Feeling safe to go ahead, we cut the tree until it fell just where we expected. The girl's reaction seemed overblown for another routine tree falling. She and the owner remained in the trailer while we cut off the limbs and stacked the resulting debris. The winds continued, but we felt no danger while continuing our efforts.

As we approached 4 p.m. the owner came out of the trailer and said we should stop for the day when we finished the tree in front of us. We presented no argument because our arms ached like crazy, and we wanted to return to our apartment before a storm blew into the area.

As we finished stacking the last logs and piling the limbs onto the ever-growing heap, the owner came over to pay us for the day's labor. The daughter remained in the trailer as we put away our tools, accepted our pay, and settled up.

"Sorry if we scared your daughter." I ventured a comment.

"It was not you, it was the trees swaying." The owner responded quickly.

He went on to explain his daughter was ten years-old when the earthquake hit. She was outside playing at a playground when it happened and one of the triggers for her memories of that day comes from tall trees swaying back and forth. The ground swells and shaking caused the trees around her playground that day to sway at exaggerated angles and it terrified her. Because she was outside during the earth quake, she avoided any falling buildings, but the memory of the trees swaying remained deep in her mind. That afternoon's wind pushing the treetops and the resulting swaying back and forth caused a panic attack for his daughter. That explained her running for the shelter of the trailer. The father quickly followed her and spent the next twenty minutes or so holding her and calming her nerves.

Our experience that afternoon gave us an item for more conversation with our co-workers when we returned to the school job. The girl's reaction to the trees swaying made quite an impression on us. Seeing the fear in the girl's eyes and hearing her shrieks made the earthquake experience very real to us. We figured anything that triggered such a reaction was a truly terrifying event.

On Monday during our morning break we asked Gabriele if she experienced the Great Alaskan Earthquake. That one simple question brought a torrent of comments from our work crew. All lived through the quake and wanted to share their experiences with us.

Gabriele told her story. That day, after finishing her work day, she drove home after stopping at Sears. She lit up with excitement while telling us she could see and feel the road rippling beneath her car. She likened it to a ride over the permafrost heaves and dips except the car was not moving, the earth was.

She also recalled the street lights swaying back and forth as the earth moved under them. She said she saw no trees, but the swaying of the street lights made her fear they would fall on her and her car.

Joe, another co-worker related how he liked to go home after work and have a drink of whiskey. He told of sitting down at his dinner table and pouring a drink of Jack Daniels when the quake struck. At first, he thought his hand was shaking but soon realized his whole house shook with the earth tremors. Other than a couple of broken windows in his house, he said the home suffered minor damage, but a house only a block away collapsed completely. He added that after the initial quake, which some estimated lasted three minutes or more, he poured a double Jack Daniels.

Three other workers joined in with their stories. A garage door thrown off its track, a wall cracking from one side of the living room to the other, a floor buckling and breaking water pipes, and the power going off across the city were among the tales we heard. Everyone expressed surprise at the quake, at first not believing it and then praying it would stop. No one expressed surprise at the girl's reaction to the swaying trees. All told of memory triggers that caused them to relive that afternoon and early evening when the earthquake hit.

As the days went by, at work and lunch breaks, we learned more about our co-workers. Some of their stories stuck with us as life's lessons learned.

Joe grew up in Idaho to a poor, farm and ranch family. He was youngest of seven children, five boys and two girls. He described his family as "Jack Mormons," a pejorative for those who rarely or never practiced the religion even though friendly toward the church. Some used the phrase to describe members who do not follow the church tenets such as prohibiting profanity, premarital sex, and the consumption of alcohol. Until Joe used the phrase neither John nor I heard it or knew what it meant. He used it with a perverse pride of authorship, something invoking praise, not condemnation. Since he talked a lot about his drinking, we assumed it meant he like to drink Jack Daniels regardless of what the Mormon church taught.

Joe migrated to Alaska with the U.S. Army during the 1950's. He claimed he always wanted to return to Idaho, but never saved up enough for the move. Others confided in us Joe always meant well, but being an alcoholic prevented many of his best intentions. We noticed over the summer, the one most likely to miss a day at work, was Joe. Joe often mentioned, and others confirmed it, that he found himself trapped in Alaska for varied reasons and could not afford to return to the Lower 48.

We heard another phrase from Joe that stuck with us. He told us, "There are two kinds of people who come to Alaska. Those who are running to something and those who are running away from something. Which kind are you?" That axiom came up several times as we met people over the summer. We joked with each other we might be running toward an adventure and did not consider the philosophical aspects of the adage until later.

## The War Bride

Gabriele gave us insight into international relations and a woman's strength. Born in Wiesbaden, Germany, she fell in love with an American G.I. after World War II. She unashamedly referred to herself as a "War Bride," but grew silent when we asked about her husband. The story went that he married her, brought her to Alaska as his next duty station, started chasing other women, and abandoned her and their marriage. She told us of wanting children but felt fortunate she ended up a family of one.

American servicemen married German women by the thousands after the war and accepted the government's promise to bring their wives and children to the United States. Gabriele thought over 20,000 German women joined her in this designation as War Brides. She saw Fort Dix, New Jersey and one afternoon in Manhattan before moving with her husband to Anchorage. The rest of the United States remained a mystery to her. She asked us a million questions about Texas. What the land looked like, did we have trees, rivers, and harbors? She wanted details about our home.

She also stood as a quiet example of strength. Even though abandoned and eventually divorced from her husband, she learned to thrive on her own terms. Because English was a second language to her, and she only had an intermediate school education in Germany, she did not qualify for many good paying jobs, but her grit and determination served her well. She worked as a housekeeper and a waitress before getting a maintenance job with the school district. At the job her innate intelligence and willingness to work soon got her promoted to a crew leader. We lucked out by joining her crew because she treated people fairly and knew how to mix encouragement with admonitions to get the most out of her workers. After a couple of weeks on the job, we decided we were her favorites because she stopped the others from assigning us the dirty, messy jobs and made sure everyone did his or her share of such jobs. We liked her.

When we learned Wiesbaden was on the Rhine River in Germany, we asked her if she knew the famous, at least to us, country and western song, "Fraulein." She claimed she did not but wanted to know more. We knew the song as a staple of country and western dances at South Plains College, where both John and I attended. First recorded by Bobby Helms, but made famous by a Hank Locklin version in 1957, we knew it well as a love song involving a German girl and an American G.I. We thought it fit the story of Gabriele's life story. At lunch the Wednesday before the July 4 holiday, everyone felt excited about the upcoming day off, and I sang it for her to everyone's delight.

*Far across the blue waters*
*Lives an old German's daughter*
*By the banks of the old river Rhine*
*Where I loved her and left her*
*But I can't forget her*
*'Cause I miss my pretty Fraulein.*

*Fraulein, Fraulein, walk down by the river,*
*And pretend you hand is holding mine,*
*By the same stars above you,*
*I'll swear that I love you,*
*You are my pretty Fraulein.*

She laughed at my singing and quickly added that no one loved her and left her until she got to Alaska, then she found herself on her own. Our coworkers smiled, but said nothing.

Paul was another part of our crew who reinforced the lessons learned from Joe. Originally from Missouri, he dropped out of school after the eighth grade and bounced around various jobs and homes across the Midwest. At age thirty, during the early 1950's he joined a work crew for a mining operation in the Yukon following a promise of good pay and adventure. Turned out he hated the twenty below zero temperatures in the Yukon, quit his job one May, and hitched a ride with a large transport headed for Fairbanks. A year or so later after finding only hand-to-mouth jobs and still very cold temperatures, he migrated south to the Anchorage area, the "Banana Belt" of Alaska and its mild climate.

He found himself in his late forties with a low-paying job and no prospects for improvement. He admired the positions in life John and I held; our futures looked promising, we were only in Alaska on a lark, and had families at home who loved us. Paul lacked all of those attributes. In addition, Paul loved beer. Ranier Beer was his weakness, probably because its price was lower than most others in the area. The west coast brewing powerhouse was based in Seattle making distribution costs a bit lower than other beers, especially compared to Paul's home-state favorite, Budweiser.

Paul liked us and we liked him, but not so much as to loan him money a day or two before payday when he continually ran short of cash. Beginning in August he quit asking, but before that we felt guilty not loaning him a ten or twenty until payday. Knowing most all things happening with her crew, Gabriele pulled us aside one day in late June and cautioned us about making any loans to co-workers. We might look prosperous, but we too, usually ran short of money before payday.

Two other ladies rounded out our work crew. Amanda and Marcie were both married with kids and needed the jobs to supplement the family income. Neither of them completed high school, both married in their teens, and seemed happy to have a job on the maintenance crews. Both married service men and found themselves stationed in Alaska. Amanda came from Ohio, her, and her husband's home state. Marcie grew up in Louisiana, met her husband in New Orleans, and followed him to Alaska. When their husband's service ended, they remained in the state. They were dependable and worked steadily, if not quickly. Everyone on the crew seemed to stay just busy enough to avoid

Gabriele's scorn and avoid any undue attention. Like Joe and Paul, they seemed resigned to a dead-end job and the idea they might never get back to the Lower 48 and their home states. Like the others the ladies admired our youth and prospects in life.

Amanda might lack a high school education, but she was a whiz with numbers. She could calculate the square footage of a room in her head while John and I were trying to walk off some measures and using the blackboards to do the math. We needed a number to allow for the quantity of floor wax required for a room and we soon learned to ask for her help. Her talents brought home the saying about the difference between education and intelligence. She did not know the House of Representatives in Washington from the House of Pies in Palmer, but her intelligence became apparent with only a few interactions.

One side benefit of being from out of state came from the others wanting to share some native food with us. Amanda and Marcie's husbands both hunted wild game and they shared deer, elk, and moose meat with us. We often fudged our assessments of the meat when asked, always praising the flavor, texture, etc. Truthfully, we did not find the wild game that appetizing, but always thanked the givers and expressed our enjoyment of the eats. Salmon, on the other hand, was a favorite. Whenever someone on the crew shared salmon steaks with us, we relished the meals and truthfully sang their praises.

That summer John and I talked a lot about the people on our crew. We admired Gabriele and her work ethic, especially after finding herself abandoned in a foreign land with few prospects. The drinking problems saddened us but also served as cautionary tales. We liked drinking beer, but saw the downside of such habits as they played out later in life. Using Amanda as an example we learned not to underestimate people who dropped out of school at an early age.

We also expressed our thanks for being in a position to know we could get home, even if it meant calling our families and pleading for money to get us there. We knew we had people who would help us in an emergency and remembered the twenty-dollar bill Cap put on the table at the Malt Shop. Feeling trapped in Alaska with no way to return home, as most of the stories of our co-workers related, was an emotion we never felt and hoped to

Charlie near small lake
in Anchorage, Alaska

never experience. We thought about those who came to Alaska running from something, who then found themselves with the same problems now compounded by circumstances they could not change. We observed many felt trapped by the vagaries of life.

Having a five-day a week job that ended at 4:30 every afternoon with hours of daylight remaining, gave us plenty of time at the end of the day and especially on weekends to explore the sights around Anchorage. John wanted to fish more, and I wanted to see everything we could. We began making plans to fill our weekends and after work hours. Our co-workers helped by suggesting hikes, short trips, fishing areas to check out, and local sights we should not miss. We did our best to fill each day to the fullest.

Our jobs provided a means to an end but also allowed us to treat every day as a holiday. Our adventure continued as we got to know our neighbors.

# Chapter 10
# The Neighbors

She was fairly attractive and very friendly; our first thoughts when we met her. She lived in the other top apartment in our building. Before we got hardly anything moved in, she came over, knocked on our doorframe, and introduced herself. She welcomed us to the building and asked several questions. She stood about five foot five inches and had a good figure. She wore her sandy-brown hair pulled back in a pony tail, had on a Mt. McKinley National Park T-shirt, and a pair of blue jeans. Being busy trying to unload the car and get our stuff situated in the furnished apartment, we briefly answered her and kept moving. We figured time for visiting with the neighbors could come later.

We learned later Wendy was married to a Navy airman stationed in the Aleutian Islands. She did not tell us that when we first met.

Our apartment was one of four in the building, an H shaped structure with two up and two down. The stairway rose to meet the crossbar in the H and supplied access to both upstairs apartments. A short, ten-foot-wide landing separated the two top apartments and the stairs' opening took up six of those. With our door open we could easily see Wendy's comings and goings, and vice versa. We closed our door, and noticed Wendy did not.

The complex had three more buildings with the same structure and floorplans. That gave us eleven neighboring apartments within a stone's throw of each other. Parking spaces occupied the front and the back yards included a bare-bones grill and picnic table for each building. It could get crowded if everyone wanted to use the grill and picnic table at the same time. As with many things in life everyone treated the grill on a first-come, first-served basis. That worked okay for us since we did little or no grilling.

Our apartment took the northeast corner of the building. This meant the rising sun shone into the two large windows on the east front. A furnished apartment at low-income housing in Anchorage in the summer of 1968 did not include window curtains or blinds. It did include a refrigerator with a small freezer section, a four-burner gas stove, and a sink. A double bed with mattress filled one room and a fold-down single bed lowered from a wall in the entrance, main room, and kitchen combination. The bathroom included a shower but no tub. A dishwasher and television did not come with the apartment. At first, we thought we might rent a television, but soon decided we needed to spend more time seeing the town and surrounding countryside than we needed a television.

We carried a small, transistor, battery operated radio with us from Texas and placed it on top of the refrigerator. The AM reception provided hourly news which kept us in touch with the world in the mornings and evenings. After the news came the Maritime Weather Report, something strange to us. Growing up in farm and ranch country we knew the early morning farm and ranch report with soil temperatures for soon to-be-planted crops, warnings against plant nematodes and root canker on already planted crops, the Fort Worth cattle prices per one hundred weight, and weather warnings for thunderstorms, dust storms, and tornadoes. No Anchorage station carried such information. Instead we got warnings of high tides, storm squalls, and general sailing and fishing conditions for the Cook Inlet, Prince William Sound, and the Gulf of Alaska from Dutch Harbor to Yakutat. Every morning we wondered where Dutch Harbor and Yakutat might be, compared to our apartment, and why we needed that information every hour. We figured those two places must be important, and somewhere near the water.

## Window Coverings

By the time we moved into the apartment, we knew in Alaska, the sun rose early and stayed around until late at night. What we did not know was what effect that would have on our sleeping habits. Because it stayed light until 11 p.m. we tended to stay up later. Our lifetime habits included waiting an hour or two after dark before going to bed. In Texas that might mean 11 p.m. in the summer and 10 p.m. or earlier in the winter. The only problem, in Anchorage, it did not really get dark, just a twilight dimming of the sunlight before the light began to increase and the sun rose, early. The first night in the apartment we finally went to bed around 1 a.m. and the 4 a.m. sunlight beaming into our windows startled us awake. At first, we thought it was time to get up, but our bodies told us otherwise. It was tough having your mind tell you it must be 10 a.m. while your body told you to get back in bed. The front room got most of the sun, but even with John closing the door to his bedroom, the light permeated his room. The morning turned bright outside, and his room also lacked window coverings. With no way to block out the sunlight, we struggled to get back to sleep. That put us on a mission to correct this unfortunate situation.

On Sunday morning, Wendy graciously showed us her window curtains and told us they were available at the local furniture and household goods store for only $150. You can imagine how we took that news. No way we planned to spend a month's rent for curtains destined to remain behind when the summer ended, and we skedaddled back to Texas. Wendy had no plan B for us. After a second morning with the sun lighting up our front room like a major league baseball park playing a night game, we knew we needed a solution.

Monday at work during our morning break we posed the question to the crew and got several answers. The ladies all suggested buying some curtains. Joe suggested taping newspaper over all the windows, but Paul discounted that idea since the newspaper would let in too much light. Instead he suggested using reflective aluminum foil. By taping the foil over all the windows, shiny side out, we could reflect most of the sunlight and some of the heat it generated. Now, six rolls of aluminum foil and some scotch tape fit our budget a lot better than fancy curtains.

After work on that Monday, and heading into our third day at the apartment we stopped and loaded up on aluminum foil at the local food mart. In less than an hour we covered every window with the foil, shiny side out. The possibility of cooling the rooms by reflecting the sun's rays did not impress us, the weather at night was mild anyway, but the possibility of darkening the interior rooms of the apartment became our main goal. That night we consciously went to bed at 11 p.m. even though it was not dark, and wished for a dark, or at least darker than the previous nights' early morning hours. It worked. I woke up around 5 a.m. with enough light to find the bathroom, but not so much I could not go back to sleep. John slept through until 7. At breakfast we marveled at how smart we became with a little help from Paul. We did not wait until the morning break, but thanked him as soon as he showed up for work, for his suggestion and lavished praise on him for the results produced. We did it all with less than $5 in materials.

Our downstairs neighbors were two married couples without children. Both men served in the service, one Air Force and one Army, one lady worked at a local bakery and the other stayed home. We got to meet them within a week of our move. Wendy, acting as social director for our building, made the introductions.

One couple represented a situation neither John nor I experienced before. We met Sandy, the wife who stayed at home, first. She was a tall, blond haired, blue-eyed, well-proportioned lady in her mid-twenties. Of course, we had the good sense not to ask her age, but she told us she and Andre got married after she finished high school and they recently celebrated their eighth anniversary. By my calculations, this made her at least 25-years-old, maybe a year or two more. I did not think she looked older than my twenty-one and a half years. She was friendly, but not as much as Wendy, and bragged about her husband when we first met her even though we did not meet him until later in the week. She went on and on about his job as an aircraft mechanic stationed at Elmendorf, how they loved living in Alaska, and she hoped we had a great summer.

Sandy told us they grew up in a small town in Kentucky, had known each other most of their lives, and how refreshing they found moving away from Kentucky. During the first years of their marriage, Edwards Air Force Base in California, was home. She let us know Andre worked on some secret airplanes there and she knew it because Chuck Yeager first broke the sound barrier in a flight from Edwards. We did not know that fact, but were impressed. They moved to Alaska two years before and had lived in the apartment for over a year.

When we met Andre a day or two later, he impressed us. Sandy came up to our apartment door one afternoon and asked if we wanted to meet her husband. She mentioned he knew some good fishing places around town and thought we would be interested. We went downstairs and she took us into the main room of their apartment. Andre came in from the bedroom and we

Charlie near small craft harbor, Anchorage, Alaska

shook hands. He just came home from the base, but looked sharp in his Air Force uniform as though he just came from an inspection. He was tall, muscular, dark haired, and ruggedly handsome. Because we met Sandy and thought she was a good-looking lady, nicely dressed, and friendly, I imagined her husband would look like someone a lady of her look and deportment might marry. Andre fit that bill. Him being Black surprised us.

John and I never met a mixed-race couple until we met Andre and Sandy. I hoped my face showed no surprise when we saw him, but he did not match my mind's image as Sandy's husband. I never imagined him as a Black man. From our experience growing up in a rural area of the south, that just did not happen. I knew the Supreme Court struck down miscegenation laws as unconstitutional the year before, but never knew anyone, especially a good-looking white woman, who married a Black man. Frankly, I never thought much about a law prohibiting interracial marriage, cohabitation, and sex. Not that I opposed it, just that I never knew anyone in that situation. Seeing Andre brought back to me what Sandy said earlier about finding it refreshing to move away from Kentucky. I could imagine what she meant.

Later John and I talked briefly about meeting Andre. His race surprised both of us. In fact, he was the first Black person we saw in Alaska, and one of the few we saw all summer. We both took sort of a "*well, this will be interesting,*" approach to living above and interacting with Andre and Sandy, wondering how they would interact with the other neighbors. I do not recall us having another conversation about the subject and they fit right in with everyone. We settled in as neighbors and came to share several times with them over the coming months.

Sandy spoke the truth, Andre knew the best fishing spots in and around Anchorage. He and John hit it off and compared notes several times over the summer. We liked both of them.

## The Friendly Neighbor

A couple of times during the summer invitations went out from our neighbors to share the table and grill behind the apartment, usually to grill some salmon Andre caught. Once Wendy invited us to share some hot dogs, so we bought some buns and joined her. We thought others might show up but the three of us made the entire picnic. We wondered why her husband was not around. Sandy had told us Wendy was married, so we asked about him. She spent some time complaining about his Navy duty out on Adak Island in the Aleutian Island chain southwest of Anchorage. The island lay almost 2,000 miles from Anchorage, a three-hour flight away. That explained why we never saw him.

We learned he served as a pilot on maritime patrol aircraft conducting surveillance of USSR naval surface ships and submarines. He flew a Lockheed P-3 Orion, four-engine turboprop, aircraft, designed for maritime patrols, reconnaissance, and submarine detection. It carried electronic equipment for magnetic detection of submarines. She related the planes often flew missions of 10 hours or more and that he served six weeks on duty and then had 10 days leave. That explained his absence. Another three weeks would pass before his next leave.

After complaining about his Navy duties, although we detected some pride in her voice explaining the importance of his service, she started complaining about him. She spoke in plain language about topics John and I felt uneasy talking with her about, mostly sex. According to Wendy, during his ten days in Anchorage all he wanted was sex, sex, sex. She bemoaned to us why couldn't he take her to a movie or out to eat? Why did he want sex in twenty or more positions over a week and a half? And, what about all the time he was away? Was ten days of non-stop sex supposed to keep her satisfied for the next month and a half? We offered no answers. Mostly, we listened. Twenty or more positions?

She complained how her husband only wanted to satisfy himself, seldom paying any attention to her needs or wants. She asked us how men could be so inconsiderate when it came to intimate relations? What happened to romance after marriage? Why was it always her job to make him happy when she got little in return? Who taught him "wham-bam-thank-you-ma'am" was the way to treat a woman? After a bit we decided she did not want us to respond, she just wanted to vent. We were good with that approach because we had no idea what to say in response. She ended the rant with some comments about divorce.

John and I both came from big families with sisters and thought we knew something about women, but Wendy's rant included things we never heard from our sisters. We made mental notes and wondered what our girlfriends might say about our romance styles. Because other than some heavy make-out sessions, we were not sexually active at that point in our lives, a lot of her complaints went over our heads. I thought about getting a book to read about twenty positions for sex.

Later, we resolved to be busy if she again asked to share the picnic table and grill. We also wondered if we might see her husband later that summer.

We lucked out with the neighbors in our building. The couple in the other lower apartment were quiet and did not interact much with the rest of us. The wife worked at a bakery and left by 4 a.m. each morning, returning mid-afternoon for a nap before greeting her husband when he returned from the Fort Richardson Army base around 6 p.m. They stayed to themselves but waved and spoke when we passed each other. We seldom heard any sounds from their apartment. The others in our building were the same. Not so for our other neighbors.

The other two buildings housed married couples, many of whom had small children. One couple in particular appeared to enjoy-suffer a tumultuous relationship. Yelling and screaming at each other was the preferred means of communication without regard for the time of day. Often late at night, we heard them arguing about money, food, the children, or the interminable sunlight of the summer months. We never observed them up close, but from the sounds of the arguments, alcohol may have been involved. Sometimes, their closest neighbors offered a screaming rejoinder commanding silence, but silence seldom arrived. In some cases, the screaming only got worse.

Colic must have been a constant companion for another couple's baby. We often heard the baby crying for what seemed like hours at a time. The parents seemed attentive when we saw them, but each night the baby tuned up, usually between 11 p.m. and midnight. Such are the pleasures of close quarter living in low-income housing units, everywhere, not just in Anchorage, Alaska.

Our building neighbors also took more pride in their living areas than others. We would win the best kept lawn award because everyone made an effort to clean up after themselves. The buildings had no lawns, just dirt in front and back. The parking held loose gravel that invariably found its way to the front yard. If we used the grill, we tried to pack away all the trash we brought with us. Those in our building obviously felt the same. We noticed the other two buildings always had trash in front and behind the apartments. No one picked up their beer cans and trash around the other buildings.

We also noticed Sandy and Andre kept a clean car and their apartment always looked neat and tidy. I could not say the same for ours although we did make an effort to empty the trash and wash the dishes every few days. We decided some people did not care about their living areas or were just too lazy to make the effort, but we felt good about our immediate neighbors.

Toward the end of August as our great adventure moved toward its closing weeks, Wendy invited us to have a drink, ostensibly to celebrate our summer and a farewell to Alaska. All summer she kept her door open and usually greeted us when we returned to the apartment. We avoided any meals or casual meetings with her. We never met her husband although we knew he was home at the end of July, first of August, because we never saw Wendy and their door remained closed for over a week.

John and I discussed whether the invitation for a drink opened us to another diatribe about her sex life. Maybe because she always greeted us and asked us to come talk to her, and we found ourselves running out of believable excuses, we agreed. We felt sorry for her. She scheduled the cocktail celebration/goodbye for a Thursday evening because we typically took off for the weekends, leaving on Friday evening.

That evening we came home from work and showered. We ate a light supper and ventured over to Wendy's around 7 p.m. Wendy left the door open, but we knocked anyway. From the bedroom or the bathroom we heard her instructions to come in. Her apartment layout mirrored ours complete with fold-out bed in the kitchen, entrance, main room. The bed hung close to the wall allowing more elbow room in the efficiency apartment.

Wendy called out, "Make yourselves at home, drinks are on the counter." The voice sounded like it came from the bathroom.

We went to the counter and saw the drinks, glasses, and an ice bucket laid out neatly on the counter. We expected beers but she had a bottle of Captain Morgan Spiced Rum on the counter. I took the task of pouring some rum and coke into glasses for us. We had our backs to the bedroom and bathroom door. As I turned to hand John a drink, I caught a glimpse of Wendy standing in the bathroom doorway. I could not believe it.

Wendy stood straight and tall, her left arm up to her head pushing her hair back, covered from the waist down with a towel, with her upper torso completely exposed. She grinned from ear to ear, winked at me and said, with sweetness dripping from her words, "I'm almost ready for you."

My mouth fell open and I quickly looked away, but not so quickly I missed a full-frontal shot of her breasts staring back at me. I turned to John and whispered, "She's naked," but by the time he turned to look she closed the door.

"What!"

"I am not kidding. She flashed me. Only a towel." I did not want to go into more details right then.

We looked again at the bathroom door and sat down on the couch, too stunned to say more. John looked at me with widened eyes as if the say, *"What the...?"*

151

We took a sip of the drinks and just sat there for a minute or two. Finally, Wendy came out of the bathroom wearing a too tight, T-shirt with "Mamma Bears Need Love Too," lettered across her boobs, which stood perfectly unencumbered by a bra. Below the T-shirt she donned a pair of short shorts designed to highlight her legs and buttocks, which they did. She walked over to the counter to fix herself a drink while making conversation about how the August days had less sunlight hours than the June days, all the while giving us a clear view of her backside. We were not thinking about the number of hours of daylight.

She turned and walked toward us and hesitated right in front of us. We had sat down next to each other, and it became clear she wanted the seat between us. I scooched over a bit while John sat perfectly still until Wendy's bottom forced him to move over. The couch was full.

"I am so glad you could come over. I wanted to give you boys a good ole Alaska sendoff before you headed to the Lower 48." Wendy acted as if she had memorized her speech.

We did not know what to say and remained quiet. I tried to ignore the image in my mind of her standing in the bathroom door with only a towel around her waist and wondered what she had in mind for the evening. Because she invited both of us, I did not expect her to try a seduction on me, John, or God forbid, the two of us. I knew of the term ménage a trois but was much too shy to consider such a thing, especially involving a good friend like John.

Wendy wore a popular perfume at the time, Jungle Gardenia. My Aunt Drucie wore the same perfume and for some reason I knew the scent. I heard, and wondered if Wendy heard the same thing, that Jungle Gardenia supposedly functioned as an aphrodisiac that attracted men. The story I heard dealt with the famous Broadway play, *Mame*, having some lines referring to the perfume, and its star, Rosalind Russell, who played up the connection. Because it reminded me of my aunt, if anything, it had the opposite effect on me. I could not imagine making out with my aunt and therefore, the scent did nothing for me.

As I sat there thinking about my aunt's perfume choice, John stood up, put his almost full drink on the counter, turned, and walked toward the door. As he left the room, he called over his shoulder, "I think I left the stove on."

That left Wendy sitting too close for comfort. I just sat there.

Wendy said something about hoping John would return soon and then hit me with a barrage of questions. Did I have a girlfriend, where did she live, how serious were we? The rapid-fire questions made me think she rehearsed them too. I stammered a few generic answers while I began to sweat under my arms. I did get out that I got officially engaged just as we left for Alaska.

A few awkward minutes followed. I realized about the same time as Wendy, John would not return.

Wendy returned to the counter for another drink. I thought she deliberately assumed the same pose as earlier when her backside was the main attraction. She took her time mixing another drink all the while slowly moving her buttocks back and forth in front of my face. Rather than exciting me, it made me even more nervous than before.

*"Thanks a lot, John. Leave me in the lurch why don't you."* I wondered why my best friend and traveling buddy abandoned me in my time of need. Actually, I wondered why I did not think of an early exit and leave him to deal with Wendy.

Wendy returned to her really close-to-me position on the couch holding her drink in her right hand. Her left arm gently settled across my shoulders as she turned and looked directly at me. I felt the sweat dripping from under both arms.

"You look like a fellow who knows how to treat a woman." Wendy said in a warm, but matter-of-fact manner. "I don't think John is coming back, maybe we can relax and enjoy the evening."

I am sure if someone took my photo right then, it would show the "deer in the headlights" look common when someone gets flummoxed. Maybe bewildered, confounded, perplexed could explain the same emotion. I felt lost.

Wendy leaned into my right side, brushing her left breast against my arm, and said she thought we might be more comfortable in the bedroom. Under other circumstances that direct invitation might sound good, but I thought of myself as engaged and not in the market for casual sex with the married neighbor. I found myself in a tricky situation with no experience about what to do next. Rather than thinking her husband might return, I wondered what I might do if John returned. Die of embarrassment, I guess.

As she stood and pulled on my arm to stand with her, I pulled back and muttered something like "you are nice and all, but I just can't do this." I walked to the door, turned, and said, "Thanks for the drink."

Our plans to explore the Russian river the next weekend supplied an easy excuse to avoid running into Wendy.

# Chapter 11
# Russian River

"Wow," was John's first reaction to seeing the water, fishermen, and red salmon jumping and swimming upstream in the Russian River. I agreed with a familiar saying in west Texas, "I've been to a goat-roping, a county fair, and inside the downtown Lubbock Woolworth's, and never saw anything like this." Our weekend at the Russian River brought many new and exciting things to our eyes.

Among the several suggestions we received when asking about things to experience during the summer in Alaska, fishing on the Russian River came up many times. The recommendation came with some caveats though. You needed to go during the salmon runs. Of course, we knew nothing about the salmon runs and needed more information. It turned out all the fishermen, including our neighbor, Andre, knew a lot about the salmon runs and enjoyed sharing their knowledge. We got the quick and dirty lesson on salmon runs, especially those on the Russian River.

I knew salmon from my mother and grandmother making what we called salmon patties. This meal involved canned salmon mixed with eggs, saltine cracker crumbs or bread crumbs as filler, and onions or garlic for flavoring. They rolled the mixture into patties and fried them in a skillet. It made for a flavorful and inexpensive dinner. Eating such patties most of my life never led me to thinking about salmon, as such. I assumed salmon was salmon, right? Apparently, not to the fishermen of Alaska.

When we asked for an appropriate time to visit the Russian River and enjoy the fishing, we ran into more questions. Did we want Sockeye or red salmon, or did we want Coho or silver salmon? We at first thought that meant four kinds of salmon, but came to understand Sockeye and red were synonymous as were Coho and silver. I did not think about a preference and John was no help, claiming he never fished for salmon. With barely felt but definitely included condescension, we got the primer on salmon from the Alaskan fishermen.

Sockeye or red salmon come from the Northern Pacific Ocean and return to the rivers discharging into it. The species turns primarily red in color during spawning, hence the name. The meat also has a reddish, orange color to it when cleaned and prepared for canning or cooking. The fish only return to fresh water to spawn and then die. Compared to a good-sized trout of one and a half to two pounds, the red salmon can grow to three feet in length and 10 to 15-pounds. The prospect of catching a 15-pound fish from a river caused John to drool with anticipation.

Sockeye or red salmon

One of the advantages of working in a school was the proximity to a library. We spent some of our lunch breaks reading up on salmon. The Sockeye or red salmon stay in fresh water near their birth until ready to migrate to the ocean, then swim to the ocean and spend two or three years, traveling over 1,000 miles, before returning to the place of their birth to spawn and die. We learned some unfamiliar words associated with the Sockeye salmon: semelparous and anadromous. Semelparous means they only spawn once, then die. Anadromous means they migrate up rivers from the ocean to spawn. Joe and Paul from our work crew knew both of those facts, but claimed they never heard those words until we said them reporting on our reading.

The savvy fishermen told us the Sockeye salmon run twice a year, in mid-June and again in mid-July. If we wanted Coho or silver salmon, we needed to wait until mid-August for their run in the Russian River.

We learned the Coho salmon had similar characteristics to the Sockeye except in the ocean they have silver sides and dark blue backs. When they return to fresh water though, their sides turn bright red and heads bluish green. The mature fish do not reach the length or weight of the Sockeye, averaging twenty-eight inches long and between 7 and 11 pounds.

When we learned the Sockeye grew larger, that cemented the idea we go during their runs. John wanted to catch as big a fish as possible and I agreed. We made plans to catch the mid-July run in the Russian River.

## A Fishing Trip

Most of our recommendations for fishing included the Russian River. Its reputation definitely preceded our visit there. We expected something extraordinary, but it turned out, we underestimated the river, and the salmon catch. The river's short length belied its reputation. It only covered thirteen miles from the headwaters to its confluence with the Kenai River and its reputation attracted a lot of fishermen. Most warned us it could turn crowded, especially on a weekend.

On a Friday afternoon, July 19th, after work, we drove out from Anchorage, along the Turnagain Arm and headed south on the Seward Highway for about an hour. We took the turn for the Sterling Highway and headed for Cooper Landing, another fifteen miles. We found several parking spaces and pulled into a camping area. We set out enough gear to establish a campsite for the next two nights and hiked from the highway to the river. It was not accessible by car.

We noticed a well-worn trail headed to the river. Within twenty minutes we reached the bank of the Russian River and its fast-flowing stream. Several fishermen were returning to the parking lot and campsites. Most carried stringers with huge fish attached. We talked to some and asked about the fishing. We learned the river regulations only allowed what they called "snagging" which meant rather than a fly or hook, the end of the fishing line carried a treble hook used to snag the fish. We also learned the experience became more like "catching" the fish than fishing, in that most fishermen, both experts and beginners, could easily catch their limit of the great tasting fish. Both of us had licenses carrying a limit of three fish per day and the news about most everyone catching fish encouraged me.

The stories sounded so good we began to think of ourselves as recipients of a good fish tale. One fisherman talked about snagging a big one who quickly headed downstream, pulling out the line as he went, then turning up stream requiring the fisherman to frantically reel in the excess line, then heading straight toward the fisherman eventually jumping right in front of him as if to show off his size. The fisherman then said the same routine repeated itself two more times before the fish tired and allowed netting. He described it as a shock and awe experience. John's eyes grew wide with anticipation, and I even began to think I might be able to snag a fish.

We passed a Fish & Game Warden who asked if we had licenses. After a quick look at ours he mentioned it was late to do any fishing that evening, but felt sure tomorrow would be good. He claimed the Russian River with its two runs of Sockeye would see 400,000 fish and even with all the fishermen, about a third of them would reach the spawning beds further upstream near the falls. He talked about how his department watched the runs to ensure good fishing for years to come and because that year's run was so deep, they allowed the snagging to help thin out some of the fish. The warden even repeated what we heard earlier, anyone should be able to catch a fish under these conditions. He reported the fish would be so thick you could see them from the banks and if you missed snagging one, another would be right behind it.

We hiked back to the campsite and prepared to get some sleep. John feared his low budget, Zebco reel and light fishing line might not live up to the task of pulling in a 12 to 15-pound salmon. I carried a cheapo fishing rod and reel, but did not have enough experience to worry about it. The warden reported most people used a 25 to 30-pound test line and our heaviest was nine. The warden favored the heavier line because of the salmon's propensity to fight and struggle against the line. He thought that the weight of the fish combined with the current of the water required the heavier line.

All of this caused John's excitement to run off the charts and even I, the poorest angler in Alaska, went to sleep with some confidence about our prospects come morning.

We ate a couple of apples and a small carton of milk for breakfast and took off. We hit the trail to the river by 6:30 a.m. and several fishermen preceded us. When we reached a good spot along the river the bank on our side contained 20 or 25 people, mostly men. Across the river stood only ten or so, but access to the other bank was not practical for us. It started three miles back with a ferry across the Kenai River just below where the Russian River joined it. Then a hike of ¾ of a mile remained to reach the bank across from where we stood. We saw fish, we guessed salmon, jumping in the middle of the river. John got right to it, but I waited on the bank to see how things went.

After working his way into a spot wide enough to allow casting 10 to 20 yards into the river, John readied his first cast. I stood several feet behind him and out of the way of his backswing, but close enough to watch. He drew back his arm and rapidly brought it forward, finishing with a quick snap of the wrist. The cast only flew a few yards in front of him. He looked back at me, paused to give each arm a windmill turn as if to warm up, and took another cast. This one landed fifteen or so yards into the river. After letting his cast stay in the flow of the river for a minute, he pulled it back and tried again. This went on for 8 or 10 casts without any luck and reminded me why I never liked fishing that much.

John, being an experienced angler, watched the others and copied their technique. Most threw their casts much like John's but then every 10 seconds or so pulled hard on the line as if trying to snag something or set a hook. John added this feature to his next cast. Within 45 seconds or so John's line started pulling away from him and his reel let out a loud whine as the line rapidly unspooled from his reel. He yelled, "I've got something," I moved down to the water's edge to watch.

Much like the stories we heard the night before, John's catch took off upstream, reversed itself and ran downstream for fifty

160

yards or so, and then headed back upstream. All the while, John struggled with the pole and tried to reel in the line whenever it showed any slack. We saw the fish jump once just a few feet in front of him and it looked enormous. I could not recall seeing a fish so big. I yelled at John to hang in there and bring him in. All of a sudden, the line went slack, and John's pole whipped back toward his body. The 9-pound test line broke. That huge fish was gone, and John's face reflected his disappointment. I looked at my watch. It was 5 minutes past 7 a.m.

John came back to the bank and reloaded a treble hook onto a new leader and attached it to his line. He smiled as he said the fish really tugged at his pole and gave him a thrill as he tried to play him into shallow water or to tire him out. I knew he enjoyed it even though he had nothing to show for it, but hey, the day was young.

"This 9-pound test line may be a problem," John's parting remark as he headed back to the water and more casting. While he reworked his rig more fishermen joined us, requiring another jostling session for a clear space to cast. Soon a fisherman appeared along the bank for every 6-foot interval. I wondered how many more fishermen might come join us, but by 7:30 the crowd stabilized, and few joined us after that.

John went back to the routine used before. The first several casts went without success, but before long, he snagged another good-sized fish. As soon as the fish realized something impeded his progress upstream, the fight was on. This time John let the fish have lots of line, sometimes to the irritation of other fishermen, because the struggle continued for several minutes and the fish took the line up and downstream, in and out, and crossed several other fisherman's lines in the water. John expertly managed this one and despite nearly every other fisherman on our side of the river getting mad at the potential for tangled lines, pulled him into shallow water and into the net. I ran to help.

John pulled a Sockeye salmon nearly 3-feet long and weighing over ten pounds out of the fabled Russian River on the Kenai Peninsula in Alaska. We thought that made it a banner day, but the other fishermen acted unimpressed.

I whacked the fish in the head with a large rock to stop its flopping around. Its size made it difficult to manage while both of us tried to hold on tight. We started to gut and clean it and realized it might take a while. The warden cautioned us the night before to put all fish waste into the fast-moving water, otherwise what to us was waste, would attract eagles or worse, bears. We brought a cooler with us, but it remained at the car, so we dressed the fish and clipped him to John's stringer and placed him in the water at the river's edge. John walked a few steps into the river and washed away the results of our gutting and trimming.

"I think the others got mad it took me so long, but I did not want to break the line again," John said to himself as much as to me. Then he asked if I wanted to try my luck. I enjoyed the morning thus far and told him I would wait until after lunch, for him to continue. He returned to the river a little after 11 a.m.

## An Unwanted Visitor

I held onto the stringer with our prized catch as John wiggled his way back to the water, working toward gaining enough elbow room to resume his casting. As we got ready to resume a quiet morning along the banks of the river, a full-blown commotion broke out on the opposite shore. All of a sudden, we saw the fishermen scurrying upstream and away from the water. Some of them broke into a run, leaving waders, extra gear, and fishing rods behind. I wondered what could cause such a ruckus when John yelled, "Look at that!" and pointed downstream. I looked and saw a large brown bear waddling up the opposite shore, pausing to scratch at and take bites from any fish he found along the way. The warden's warning materialized in the hulking bear hardly fifty yards away. Luckily, the bear showed much more interest in the fish left behind than in the fishermen.

All the fishermen vacated the premises with what an English professor might say, alacrity. None waited to greet the bear. Our side of the river stood still, closely watching the bear. No one moved or made a sound. We all watched as the bear ambled up and down the river's bank searching for fish.

The bear took his time about wandering the other shore and checking out the easy pickings of fish on stringers left behind. He stopped and ate several, tearing them apart with his powerful claws and then biting into the resulting chunks of salmon meat. A few times he looked over at our side, but made no moves to cross or enter the river. Most everyone remained stock still and watched his every move.

After ten minutes or so, with the bear still rummaging up and down the opposite shore, some of the fishermen on our side resumed casting. They did so with one eye constantly returning to the bear. No one saw any fishermen on the other shore. They disappeared, and if they watched the bear as we did, it came from a well camouflaged location. I had a hunch they were at least ¼ of a mile upstream.

We decided to take a lunch break and talked about the excitement of the morning. John had caught a huge salmon, and we avoided a bear making a meal of us. We laughed that those were two experiences no one ever, since the beginning of time, experienced in Cochran County, Texas and we still had a day and a half remaining to the weekend.

By the time we finished lunch the bear wandered away. The fishermen returned half an hour later, slowly looking around as they crept back. We watched as they inspected the bear damage to their fish stringers and reassembled their gear. A few waved at us when they saw us watching them from our, safe side, of the river. It occurred to me, seeming that the bear made easy pickings of the other bank, he might cross the river and easily repeat his performance on our side. I resolved to keep an eye out for the bear. John surmised the bear ate so much he would take an afternoon nap. I sure hoped so.

John offered me a chance at the salmon, and I prepared my gear. He talked about pulling on the line every few seconds to snag a fish. He acted like there were so many salmon in the river, I could not miss. I laughed and told him he already knew what a poor fisherman I was, but maybe I could get lucky with 400,000 fish swimming in front of me.

My first few casts fell short of the goal, but I improved after a bit and got the hook out to mid-river. My first several casts produced nothing, in fact, I saw the afternoon passing without snagging anything. John kept encouraging me to stick with it.

Finally, I snagged something that took my line and flew away. I felt the strong tug from the line at my pole, surprised at the fish's strength as it tried to escape. John urged me to hold on tight. I tried, but did not allow enough slack to the line and it snapped, just like earlier.

As we rigged another treble hook onto my line, John told me how my luck had improved and next time, I would bring one home. I was not so sure, but remained willing to try again. After a few minutes, I began wiggling my way into a spot along the shore.

Before the end of the afternoon I proved myself a great salmon fisherman. I snagged two big, but not as big as John's first catch, salmon, and brought them to the net after some struggle. I did not break the line any more, and felt great about the success. I offered to clean them and let John get back to fishing.

164

We each had a limit of three, and our catch thus far, when combined, left one for me and two for John. I told him to stay with it until he caught my limit and his. We figured the warden would not object as long as we had six between us.

By late that afternoon we had our six salmon and fifty pounds of fish. At the campground we talked with another angler who showed us how to filet the salmon and carve them up into steaks about 6 inches wide by 4 inches deep, each about 2 to 3 inches thick. We worked for over an hour cutting up the fish and placing them in our cooler. We then made a quick campfire and fried up two of the steaks. Maybe it was the thrill of the hunt, or the fresh, clean air of the campsite, but whatever the reason, that night we

Sockeye salmon filets-steaks
Photos courtesy of Alaska Department of Fish & Game

ate the best tasting salmon steaks EVER! It was good we enjoyed the taste because we would soon have plenty of salmon to eat before heading home.

On Sunday, I let John do the fishing and he caught our limit of six by 2 p.m. I cleaned, filleted, and packed the catch away and we headed home by 4:30, content with our successful trip to the Russian River. With this experience under our belts we felt like real, experienced Alaskan fishermen, although John laughed that next time, he would pack 30-pound test line and avoid the fish breaking our lines and escaping. I was just thrilled with a catch even though the snagging did not take much skill, getting those beauties to the shore did.

We arrived at the apartment around 7 p.m. and began wrapping the salmon steaks in aluminum foil, usually 2 or 4 steaks to a wrapping. In 1968 the vacuum sealed plastic wraps and self-sealing bags were not widely available, so aluminum foil became the wrapper of choice. We packed into the freezer compartment of our refrigerator every pound of salmon it would hold. We took out the ice trays to give us room for two more salmon steaks. Our standard size refrigerator held nowhere near the capacity we needed, so we knocked on Wendy's door, and she let us stash six or seven steaks in her freezer despite my quick departure the last time we were together. We went downstairs to see Andre and Sandy who graciously let us store more salmon steaks in their freezer. We promised them a steak or two for their generosity and returned to our apartment.

Back in our apartment, we sat on the couch and drank a couple of beers while reliving the weekend. Pretty soon we believed we ranked among the greatest salmon fishermen in the world because we gathered forty pounds or so of Sockeye/Red Salmon steaks. After several minutes of self-congratulatory remarks, John said, "How are we going to eat 40 pounds of salmon in the next month?"

I had no answer. For the first time wondered why we brought home so much. We talked about giving some to our co-workers, to Richard and Betty, maybe some to the fellow building the house, and of course, our neighbors who let us store some in their freezers. With our quick calculations we figured we could pass around twenty pounds or so. That left plenty for us.

Over the next several weeks, we explored many ways to eat salmon. A salmon steak supplied a generous portion for one, so we usually thawed and cooked two at a time. We fried and grilled steaks, we baked some, we considered smoking some, but had no equipment, and we broke the baked steaks into large pieces and used them in salads. We ate fried salmon with eggs for break-fast, placed some between bread slices and ate salmon sand-wiches for lunch, and we ate some cold cuts with toast for breakfast. We even considered salmon with raisin bran cereal, but passed on that idea.

The first week after our fishing trip we ate salmon six con-secutive days. It tasted great and supplied us with a healthy sta-ple. Salmon comes naturally free of carbohydrates, including fiber and sugar, and provides omega-3 fatty acids which we learned were healthy. Wild salmon, like our stash, is leaner than mass produced salmon in farms, but we did not exactly watch our weight that summer. One portion gave us protein, vitamin A and multiple B-vitamins, and vitamin D, so we felt eating that many fish made us some of the healthiest people on earth. We slowed the pace some in the coming weeks, but still ate salmon 3 or 4 times each week thereafter. All that eating did produce one negative aspect.

After a month of trying to eat through our salmon, we began to taste salmon in everything; milk, water, coffee, beer, Coca-Cola, you name it. Everything brought the salmon taste to our mouths. We began to long for a good old-fashioned T-bone or Ribeye beef steak. Instead we still had several pounds of salmon in our freezer and were yet to take any we had stashed with our neighbors.

We did take several steaks to co-workers and Richard and Betty. We donated more to our neighbors and still our freezer contained salmon. The day we left the apartment we asked Wendy to take or dispose of the last two salmon steaks in our freezer.

I to this day love salmon, but try to eat it once or twice a month instead of once or twice a day for 40 days.

# In the Land of the Midnight Sun

# Chapter 12
# Trip to Seward

We asked everyone we saw what sights in Alaska we should not miss. Having the weekends off and good transportation, at least on the main roads, gave us two full days to explore areas within a reasonable drive of Anchorage. Reasonable is a fluid term, when you consider two young men who drove 600 and 700 miles a day to reach the 49th State. Those daily mileage tallies might not seem reasonable or safe to our mothers, but we did them in our eagerness to reach Alaska. We figured anything within a three-hour drive made for a weekend opportunity.

Most people we encountered at work, at casual meetings at a restaurant, and a few times, in the checkout line at the supermarket, gladly gave us suggestions. Matanuska Glacier came up several times. Been there, done that, on the way to Anchorage. Other popular destinations were Homer, at the end of the Kenai peninsula, and Mt. McKinley National Park. Homer lay 226 miles southwest of Anchorage with a paved road all the way. Most people cautioned it needed a three- or four-day turnaround. Five hundred miles in two days left little time for sightseeing, especially when construction and repairs from the earthquake slowed traffic on long sections of the road. Mt. McKinley National Park offered two access routes, the railroad and highway.

Railroad tickets often booked solid months in advance and the highway required a circuitous route. We considered trying to drive to the park until we realized it required over four hundred miles one way. In 1968 the current road from Anchorage to the park existed only in a tour planner's dream. The road in those days went a few miles past Talkeetna then came to an abrupt halt. It followed the railroad route, but remained unfinished. This fact allowed the quickest way to reach the park by backtracking our way to Palmer, then Glennallen, then north to Paxson, then west to the park. The idea of traveling over eight hundred miles in a weekend and seeing the park oh, so briefly, did not overcome our practical side. These daunting logistics marked both Homer and McKinley off the wish list and made us appreciate the enormity of the state. Besides, on a cloudless day one could see Mt. McKinley from Anchorage. It loomed white and shiny from the ice fields and glaciers on its upper levels and stood prominently on the horizon on the rare, good visibility days. Most often, clouds obscured the summit, but when visible, it presented a grand sight. Because we experienced a few such days, we could truthfully say we saw Mt. McKinley.

Seward got several recommendations. It got its name from the U.S. Secretary of State, William H. Seward, who forged the purchase of Alaska from Russia back in 1867. For many years, the territory took on pejoratives such as, "Seward's Folly," and "Seward's Ice Box," but by the twentieth century the purchase price of $7.2 million dollars, or less than 2 cents per acre, proved a spectacular bargain purchase.

The town sits at the head of Resurrection Bay, at the north end of the Gulf of Alaska and the northern Pacific Ocean. The Russian explorer, Alexander Baranov, gave the bay its name after he retreated into the bay during a storm and the storm passed on Easter Sunday.

Seward nestles into the surrounding mountains, glaciers, and open water revealing a spectacular setting. The Sterling highway, Alaska Route 9 connects the town to Alaska Route 1 running from Anchorage to Homer at the end of the Kenai Peninsula. The Alaska Railroad follows the same route to its southern terminus at Seward. The highway provides beautiful scenery in all directions and received a solid surface in 1954. Workers completed repairs necessitated by the earthquake in mid-summer 1968 which also made the route attractive to us. One of its salient advantages: only 128 miles separated it from Anchorage. Even with sightseeing along the way, we could cover the distance in 3 hours, easy. We made plans to visit.

We planned the weekend several days in advance and stocked up with bread, some eggs, mixed nuts, apples, and beer to go with our ever-popular Vienna Wieners. Early on a Saturday morning in August, like 5 a.m. early, John drove as we left Anchorage headed south to the northern side of Turnagain Arm and its panoramic views of the Chugach Mountains on the Kenai Peninsula. My job was map reader, navigator, and keeper of the Milepost guidebook.

We saw several glaciers hanging from the mountain sides and enjoyed the sunlight reflecting off the muddy waters in the arm. About thirty-five miles from town we passed Girdwood, a town devastated by the earthquake and the tsunamis it produced. The devastation required the town to move to higher ground. We saw where acre after acre of land subsided causing the water to rush in, killing the trees. Treetops stood several hundred yards out into the water and some abandoned buildings remained half buried in the silt. The area took on the characteristics of a ghost town.

A few miles further we reached the end of Turnagain Arm at the Portage Glacier and the remains of its namesake town. It, too, received great damage from the earthquake. The recently re-paired roadway took us to a turnout where we saw the railroad branch line turn east toward Whittier, another ice-free port on the northwest end of Prince William Sound. We looked for signs of Dutch Harbor or Yakutat, the two names we heard often on the radio's maritime reports. We did not see any.

From there we turned south still on Alaska Route 1. We saw Portage and Twenty-Mile Glaciers in the distance. The ice and snowcapped peaks offered a brilliant contrast to the wild flowers, mountain hemlock, and spruce trees spread across the valley floor

Charlie on the icefields near Seward

and part way up the mountain sides. John remarked how much different it looked from the trips we took in our teens to Post, Texas, and its Boy Scout camp just below the Caprock. The Mile-post guidebook showed the flowers included False Azalea, yellow and purple violets, Mt. Heliotrope, Louseworts, Paintbrush, and several kinds of blue-berries. John gave me a weird look and asked what a Lousewort looked like. I had no clue and unfortunately, the guidebook showed no pictures.

Twenty miles further we came to the junction for Moose Pass and Seward and turned east. The junction supplied the route to Hope, the site of a placer gold stream on the southern shore of Turnagain Arm. It flourished in the 1890's with Alaska's first gold strike—the Klondike strike came in the Yukon of Canada. Many fortune seekers reached the gold fields via Skagway, Alaska, and some made their way to Hope. In 1968 Hope only provided a nice historic site for a picnic and little else.

By 9 a.m. we reached the junction of Alaska Routes 1 and 9, and turned southeast toward Seward. At Moose Pass we stopped for some coffee and to stretch. The guidebook showed the elevation at the pass only reached 533 feet which did not seem like much to us, but it made the mountain tops surrounding us seem to jut into the sky before reaching their 4,500 to 5,000 feet elevations. The dra-matic gain in elevation to the mountain sum-mits created an environ-ment we guessed similar to the Alps in Switzer-land. We sat on the car fenders, drank our cof-fee, and soaked up the magnificent vistas in all directions. We saw sev-eral alpine glaciers clinging to the moun-tainsides all around us.

John on the icefields near Seward

We resumed our journey a few minutes later and came to parallel Kenai Lake for several miles. The lake looked more like a glacier, but at the south end we saw the milky blue color of the glacial water flowing from the lake. Before long we crossed the Resurrection River and could see the bay and Se-ward down the valley.

173

## Visiting Seward

The sun peeked in and out of the clouds as we drove into town to take a look around. We found a town about the population of Morton, 3,000 or so people, on a narrow, level strip of land with mountainsides coming down to within city blocks of the bay. The waterfront infrastructure looked new, rebuilt after the earthquake. A small boat harbor stretched out into the water. Several people in their boats were moving in and out of the harbor. A few blocks away a larger harbor hosted larger boats unloading at the fish canneries. Seward hosted a fish freezing plant for frozen salmon and halibut steaks. One of the delicacies from the plant was red caviar. All of the fish products shipped from Seward, mostly to the west coast of the U.S., but some to Japan.

We ate at a harbor front restaurant featuring Pacific salmon steaks and chowed down with some enthusiasm since our budget would require our own cooking for the rest of the weekend. The waterfront bustled with tourists, fishermen, boaters, and workers from the close-by canneries. John asked me, as we enjoyed our salmon steaks, if I had seen anyone I knew that morning. The answer stayed the same as it had for the past several weeks.

We visited Seward in August, but the town still had posters and banners advertising the 4th of July endurance race to the top of Mt. Marathon. World class athletes competed in the grueling race to the top of the mountain, 4,826 feet above sea level. The race started in downtown Seward and traveled about three miles to the summit with an average steepness of 34°. We talked about how steep, or level, 34° might be and moved our hands up and down to estimate the change from level to a position of 45° and decided 34° was plenty steep. We had no desire to climb Mt. Marathon, but it did give us an idea.

John wanted to get in some fishing, and the weather looked reasonable, so we traveled out of town and up the Resurrection River valley. We found several creeks joining the river and a few small lakes in and around the river valley. We knew Seward's renown for Silver or Coho salmon, King salmon, Pink or hump-back salmon, halibut, and various species of rockfish, hence the canneries, but those all came from saltwater. Lacking the equipment, time, or money to hire a boat and guide for ocean fishing, we stuck to the freshwater fish.

The guidebook showed wild rainbow trout and Dolly Varden should be available along with stocked lake trout and Arctic grayling. John's experience fit right in with the rainbow and lake trout, but he figured he could catch anything, and he did. Before evening he caught several trout and a couple of Dolly Varden. I served as chief fish cleaner and camp builder. We found a level spot near a little lake and set up for the night. I constructed a rock fire pit for cooking and gathered enough wood for a campfire. When John stopped by with a stringer of fish, I told him to keep it up and I would clean his catch. He grinned and returned to the task.

Early on we worked out a division of labor for our chores and camping. Since I lacked any expertise for fishing, and really did not enjoy it that much, we agreed he should do what he did best and catch the fish. I did not mind setting up the camp and tending the fire. The fish cleaning was not my favorite task, but it led to good eating. I spent the leisure time hiking a short distance from the car while enjoying the scenery and daydreaming about how the pioneers had a tough go of things. Living in the wild overnight struck me as a lot easier than making a home in the wild for months or years at a time, especially the winter months, which I could only imagine.

We enjoyed our meal of fresh fish rolled in cornmeal and cooked in a frying pan. John supplied enough fish for each of us to eat three. Each one weighed a couple of pounds, allowing plenty of meat from each fish even after the cleaning. The pan only held two good sized trout, so it took a few rounds to get through the entire catch. John did the fish frying, and I tended a small saucer of beans. The fish, beans, and two beers for each of us made for two satisfied campers that night.

Before darkness set in around 10:30 p.m. we saw clouds rolling in and hoped to avoid any rain. We took notice of the clouds and light rain that often accompanied the coastal areas, noting much more frequent rain than we experienced during west Texas summers. Mostly, we did not want to sleep in the Pontiac. We experienced enough of that on the way north. Luckily, we made it through the night without rain.

When we awoke around 6 a.m. on Sunday, the cloud cover was solid and the temperature much cooler than when we went to sleep. John felt satisfied with his fishing time from the day before and given the weather, suggested we go for a hike before heading back to Anchorage. While discussing the Mt. Marathon endurance race earlier, we talked about hiking up it or one of the other mountains and looking down on the city and the surrounding area. We agreed to that as the activity of the day.

Too lazy to build a fire and cook eggs, our breakfast consisted of an apple and mixed nuts. I declined John's offer to break out the Vienna Wieners. We loaded the car and drove back to Seward. The clouds became darker, and some misty rain began as we got into town. We surveyed Mt. Marathon, but decided it looked too steep for a casual hike. One of the other mountains next to the port offered what looked like an easy alternative, one that showed some elevation gain and good views of the town and bay. It lay to the north of town and the road went right by the base of the mountain. We drove about five miles and found a hiking trailhead. We pulled onto a gravel bar that served as an unofficial parking lot in that three other cars beat us there. The rain turned to sleet as we started up the trail. We wondered if it might snow in August.

Sure enough, after hiking half an hour we got a beautiful view of the town and the bay even though the clouds continued to hang low over our heads. The sleet let up a little, but we kept our rain gear on. At that point, the trail turned to snow and ice. We had neither crampons nor snow shoes, so our progress slowed considerably. We joked about being great explorers headed onto a glacier. Despite the rain gear, the chilly air and damp conditions made us wonder how smart we were heading up an ice field in the sleet and cold. It reminded us of the great distance between us and the August heat of Texas. We decided to take some photos and head back to the car.

Because of the early start, we decided enough daylight remained, one of the benefits of the longer daylight, that we could backtrack to the junction of Alaska Route 1 and 9 and head southwest toward Soldotna. There was time to check it out before heading to the apartment. We knew Homer, at the end of the Kenai peninsula, lay too far away, but the small town of Sterling was along the route, only seventy miles or so from Seward. We started driving toward Sterling.

As we got away from the fjord and Resurrection Bay and headed into the Chugach Mountains the rain/sleet let up and the heavy cloud cover lessened considerably. By the time we reached Sterling it was early afternoon and cloudy, but no rain. That route took us down from the mountains and onto a broad coastal plain where the geography looked very different from the icy snow fields, we left only a couple of hours before. Instead of the mountains coming right down to the water's edge like Seward, here the land opened up with only a rolling plateau stretching from the mountains to Cook Inlet and the sea. John said this looked to him like good fishing country.

## Fishing on the Moose River

At Sterling, an unincorporated village of maybe five hundred people, the Moose River runs into the Kenai River and both loop around in horseshoe bends as they snake their way to the sea. Both flowed with good streams of water, but not the rushing flows we saw in June.

The town included a couple of stores and a gas station. The Sterling Sausage Company caught our eye. They advertised smoking and canning for your fish and touted their reindeer sausage. John said that must mean lots of fish occupy the streams around there. We started looking for a good spot to fish. We had no reindeer meat to offer the sausage company.

We turned north and drove up the Moose River valley a few miles until John pulled off the highway and announced we found a good fishing hole. The East Fork of the Moose River headed back to the northeast and after parking the car, we started walking a bit upriver. This time because the river looked tame enough to me, I decided to do a little fishing. My decision surprised John, as we both attacked the stream to try our luck. He declared it was not too late for me to become a fisherman, but his remarks did not bolster my confidence.

The landscape included a few scraggly looking trees taller than a man, but most of the trees were waist high. A forest fire along this section of the Moose range in 1947 burned thousands of acres. The effects of the fire were still evident twenty-one years after the fire. The short trees represented the new growth and gave evidence of how long it takes, given the shortened growing season, to grow a mature tree on the Kenai peninsula.

Before we left the car, we pulled off our raingear and changed to lighter clothing to match the change in the weather. It amazed us how quickly the weather could change by driving an hour or so. I put on a hooded sweatshirt and donned a western style cowboy hat. We wondered how many Texans visited Sterling each summer.

John pulled a trout out of the water within minutes. After half an hour with no luck, I asked what I did wrong, but he just grinned at me and kept fishing. I tried to match his every move, but my fishing luck was all bad. I did get a couple of nibbles which only encouraged me to keep at it. John caught four or five good sized trout before I pulled out a little bitty trout that resembled a minnow. John was so impressed, he dropped his fishing rod and took my photo. He joked about how I should

Charlie's Trophy Catch
on the East-Fork Moose River, Alaska

have it stuffed and mounted over the fireplace mantel at the Ledbetter homestead. I was impressed that I at least caught something, but threw the little fellow back after we took the photo.

We spent another two hours fishing along the river. John's skill stood out, as usual, and I, to my great relief, caught one more rainbow trout. He caught three more. That raised another problem. We brought no ice or a cooler with us to keep the fish while we drove the two and a half hours back to Anchorage.

We stopped at the gas station and filled the tank. The man filling the tank, yes, in those days an attendant handled those duties, noticed the Texas license plates on the car. He asked how we got the Pontiac all the way to Sterling, Alaska. That started a repeat of a conversation we held several times over the past months. When we talked about the ferry ride, he perked up and asked several questions about how it managed cars, etc. He related how he was Alaskan born and raised so we did not get to ask him what he was running from or to. His interest in the ferry stemmed from a wish to visit a cousin in Vancouver, British Columbia. We told him we did not travel to Vancouver and could not help with that segment of the trip, but related how we found the ferry easy and convenient. We also told him we slept most of the ride north to Haines.

Our talk about the trip north and the ferry ride evoked some sympathy for us. After he heard of our fishing success and the pending journey back to Anchorage, he gave us a plastic bucket for our fish. We told him a trip back to return the bucket was unlikely and he waived us off; his way of saying, "Don't worry about it." We talked about how friendly folks seemed when they heard about our trip from Texas to Alaska. Earlier in the summer we joked about this and considered opening every conversation with, "And, we drove all the way from Texas to Alaska in this Pontiac." This person proved the point with his generosity. Unfortunately, he had no ice, so we filled the bucket with stream water, added the cleaned fish and started home. Only problem came from keeping it from sloshing over. John insisted on driving, and I understood why when he suggested rather than putting it on the floor of the car, I hold the bucket in my lap all the way home.

We retraced our steps to Portage at the head of Turnagain Arm where we knew the rest of the way without looking at the map. The sun hung low on the horizon and low tide in the arm revealed several mud banks and silt bars.

We pondered if Captain Cook saw it at low tide, surely there was no way he authorized a venture to explore it, it lacked enough water for anything but the smallest boats. With the sun reflecting off the sand and ribbons of water, we felt tired, but satisfied with our weekend outing.

We made it to the apartment without one slosh from the bucket onto my lap. The fish went in the crowded freezer compartment with what remained of the salmon.

We arrived in time for bed by 11 p.m., just as sky grew dark and could not wait to tell the work crew of our trip to Seward and a side trip to Sterling. I thought I might even brag about catching a fish. After that successful weekend, and with only a few weekends remaining in our summer, we planned to ask for more recommendations of places to visit before September arrived.

In the Land of the Midnight Sun

# Chapter 13
# Kodiak

Kodiak often came up when we asked about places to see in Alaska. We asked if they meant the town or the island, or both. The island received the most comments. Because we could not drive there, we never seriously considered it. Getting a car to the island involved two or three ferry rides and a full day's journey. With those limitations, no way could we get there and back over a weekend. Then we heard an advertisement on the radio about a Native Alaskan Fair featuring an outdoor theater presentation of *Russia in Alaska*. Attendance fees for anyone coming from Anchorage included a group airfare of $50 round-trip. Such a bargain fare intrigued us, and we began to check it out.

Several people suggested the island as a place to visit because of its unique features. The town of Kodiak lies at the eastern end of Kodiak Island, an island over one hundred miles long with varying widths from ten to sixty miles. The island ranks second in size to all islands in the United States, behind Hawaii, the big island in the Hawaiian chain. It is on the western side of the Gulf of Alaska and separated from the Katmai Peninsula on the mainland by the Shelikof strait. This separation provides one of the distinguishing characteristics of animal life on the island, the Alaskan Brown Bear or Kodiak bear.

Once the ice sheets of the last Ice Age melted some 10,000 to 12,000 years ago, the island's bears became genetically isolated. Since then the bears supplied future generations little genetic diversity and the result produced a subspecies of the brown bear known for its enormous size. The Kodiak bear is one of two sub species of the brown bear, the Grizzly bear the other. Because of the abundant food sources and no indigenous threats other than humans, the Kodiak bears grew and grew until they became outsized compared to all other bears except the Polar Bear.

Kodiak bear

Photo courtesy of KodiakIsland.com

The bears typically stand four-foot, nine-inches tall at the shoulder with four feet on the ground and when standing upright often reach nine to ten-foot high at the crown of the skull. Although cubs weigh less than one pound at birth, an adult female often weighs between 250 and 750 pounds, and an adult male can weigh 650 to 1,350 pounds. The bears are so big it is hard for humans to understand.

Baylor University owned several generic brown bears one finds in the Lower 48 states. The bears we saw at football games were nowhere near the size of the Kodiak bear. Baylor's bears stood six-foot six-inch upright and weighed 250 pounds. They often showed a playful nature and upon command, drank Dr Pepper from a bottle. I found it hard to imagine a bear's head scraping the bottom of a basketball goal and weighing over 1,200 pounds, but figured it would be fun to see such a creature, alive or stuffed.

The other native to Kodiak Island, and a distinguishing feature, was the red or king crab. It is commercially viable in Alaskan waters and the most prized of the crab types for its meat. The Kodiak archipelago hosts many large commercial crab fishing operations. The red king crab found in these waters is the largest of the species, reaching a carapace width of eleven inches and a leg span of six feet. A mature male can weigh twenty-eight pounds although the typical male weighs in closer to six and a half pounds. The crab is pinkish in color while in the

Alaskan red or king crab,
native to waters near Kodiak Island
Photo courtesy of KodiakIsland.com

ocean, but takes on the reddish color when cooked.

In addition to the bears and king crab, Kodiak island presents misty fjords and rugged mountains. Clouds often sock-in the island and rainfall comes often. This combination of factors, rugged beauty and foggy-rainy weather gives the island an almost mystical quality. If we could get there and back for $100, it sounded pretty good to us. We called the number advertised.

# A Weekend In Kodiak

The promotion included the airfare from Anchorage, only 250 air miles to the town of Kodiak. It left on a Saturday morning and returned Sunday afternoon with the open-air theater presentation on Saturday evening, come rain, or shine. The price did not include meals or a place to stay overnight, but by this time in the summer, sleeping out in a park or campground deterred us not in the least. We thought of ourselves as seasoned outdoors men by mid-July, tempered only by the memory of the giant mosquitoes chasing us into the car while making an overnight stay in the Yukon. Regardless of any dangers present on Kodiak Island, we wanted to make the trip.

Early on that Saturday we headed to the airport. We experienced some second thoughts when checking in at the small, private airline Quonset hut office. Behind the office stood a single-engine, old-fashioned, bush plane with a camouflage coat of paint. My first thought was of surplus WW2 aircraft Eisenhower used to cross the channel on D-Day. We were not impressed with the tail dragging, single engine plane with a long wing fixed across the top of the fuselage. We later learned it was a distinctive design by the British de Havilland company for STOL (short takeoff and landing) planes. In fact, the plane used a war-surplus 450 hp Pratt & Whitney engine for extra power to go with the long wing in an effort to maximize its STOL performance. Bush pilots in Alaska often equipped these planes with wheels, skis, or floats, allowing them to take off and land in remote areas lacking paved runways. Ours had wheels so we assumed Kodiak's airport featured a runway.

The unassuming looks to the plane signaled its duty as a working aircraft for flights in rugged and remote areas. It had a full-sized door on each side, allowing for cargo. Instead of cargo, this plane's configuration allowed for six people: the pilot and five passengers. We learned nothing that clarified its camouflage paint job. Maybe it planned to sneak up on the bears—one of our thoughts. We took note of three persons in the small office waiting instructions about the flight to Kodiak.

Soon the pilot appeared. He stood five foot, ten inches and sported a bushy beard. I thought the beard's purpose was to cover up his boyish looks. We figured twenty-five years-old, but he spoke confidently about the plane and our flight to the island. Partly cloudy weather prevailed in Anchorage, and he said it should be clear most of the flight. We felt a little better about climbing into this strange looking craft after his talk.

The pilot looked over the passengers and assigned seats. A woman weighing 120 pounds joined him up front in the shotgun seat, John and I took the middle seats, and two men joined us in the last row of seats. Only the pilot had a headset, helmet, and mouthpiece, but everyone could see out the windows. I settled in and tried to set aside my uneasiness about the plane.

We taxied out to the runway, got clearance, and took off. The pilot pushed the engine full throttle and we rolled down the runway, slowly at first, and then faster and faster. We traveled less than one hundred yards before the plane rose, the wheels left the ground, and we began a steep climb away from Anchorage. After such a short takeoff, I feared we might fall back to earth. The pilot maintained a steep climb for the first three or four minutes then began to level off. My first experience with STOL aircraft started well.

We flew west out over the Cook Inlet then turned southwest along the Kenai Peninsula staying over water for the first part of the flight. To our left we saw the snowcapped Chugach Mountains and the broad coastal plain of the peninsula. The engine whirred loud in our ears so we could not talk much, but enjoyed beautiful views. The sun and patchy clouds made for a wonderful day of flying.

We flew at the relatively slow speed of 125 mph while maintaining an altitude of 10,000 feet. Once we reached our cruising speed and altitude, the plane ride became smooth and enjoyable. The pilot motioned to point out Homer, the last town at the end of the highway near the foot of the peninsula. Soon we left the land behind and saw only the ocean below. We passed a couple of small islands dotting the water as we continued to the southwest.

Afognak Island came into view after an hour and a half. The pilot signaled as we passed over it and pointed toward our destination, the next large land mass, Kodiak Island. He made a turn to the south and then a U-turn back north as we approached the airstrip. The plane came in for a perfect landing, no bumps, jumps, or skips. Soon after, we taxied to a small terminal and deplaned.

Inside the terminal we got a dose of the Kodiak experience. Just inside the building stood a full-grown, standing exhibit of the famous Kodiak bear. I am sure my mouth fell open when I saw it, right after John punched me in the arm. He did not want me to miss the exhibit. No way anyone, other than a blind man, missed this work of taxidermy. It towered over all of us mortals by three or four feet. Its huge paws with four-inch-long claws, extended from its body in a menacing manner. The bear's mouth gaped to show its formidable teeth and red tongue. The bear stood positioned such that women and small children might cringe at its presence. John and I stood still and looked him over from top to bottom. I tried not to think about it chasing me.

If the exhibit's designer wanted to make a lasting first impression, he achieved that in spades. I could not remember seeing an animal, other than an elephant at Ringling Bros., Barnum & Bailey's circus, anywhere as large as this bear. We discussed how others told us about the huge size of the Kodiak bears, but we agreed they undersold the impact the sight had on us.

My college basketball experience put me around some outsized men, some six foot, ten-inches tall or so, but most were thin. I once rode the elevator with a seven-foot-tall basketball player, but at best, he weighed 250 pounds. By comparison, this bear's girth was as impressive as its height. Its massive hulk left a lasting impression on me. Enormous does not begin to describe it. We hung around a few minutes, like all the passengers, just staring at the bear.

The promoters arranged a minibus to take us into town about two miles to the east, so we loaded in for the short ride. The pilot thanked all of us and told us he would return on Sunday afternoon for our flight back to Anchorage. Judging from the activity at the small office, only two passengers appeared ready to join him for his return flight.

We reached the small town, approximately 2,500 population, by early afternoon and ate lunch at a small café. The café had two specials that day, King crab and salmon fillets. We chose hamburgers instead. We inquired about a campground or hostel and got our bearings for the amphitheater. The scheduled performance for Russia in Alaska was seven hours away, so we had the afternoon to find a place to spend the night, check out the festival, and get to the amphitheater.

The small harbor centered the town. The few roads led to and from the harbor, each with businesses, fish shops, tourist stands, and cafés filling the city blocks. A large cannery sat back a couple of blocks from the water, but had a short railroad line running from it to the docks. We assumed the line allowed movement of heavy loads of fish or king crab from the dock. The Native Alaskan Fair featured banners and posters around the town advertising the festivities. Other than the temporary stands put up for the festival, Kodiak looked like a working town to us.

## Russians in Alaska Pageant

We learned the Alutigg peoples lived on the island for at least 7,000 years. The information booth presented a story of the original people arriving by foot when the ice caps extended from the mainland to the island. This same idea applied to the native people populating North America beginning 12,000 to 15,000 years ago, they just walked over from Siberia. We enjoyed looking at the exhibits and learning more about the area and its history.

We learned quite a bit from the exhibits at the festival, but the full-blown story of Russian exploration came with the evening performance. After reserving a camping space, we walked to the outdoor theater and settled in for the show. The production played out on a mountainside on the north side of town. Slit log construction made up the seats with the logs anchored into the hillside. The stage came with flood lights and spotlights allowing us to see the actors even though the twilight darkness common between 9 p.m. and 11 continued past the show's end. The performance took place on the open-air stage with lots of extras coming and going on the stage. It had battles, explorations, and lots of fur trading. It also overlooked many of the sordid details of the Russian treatment of the native people of Alaska. The performance reiterated some of what we learned earlier, but focused on the Russian experience in Kodiak and Alaska.

For thousands of years the native people lived undisturbed, but we learned the Russians and the British began arriving in the late 18th century. Kodiak island first appeared in a log of Stephan Glotov, a Russian explorer, in 1763. The renowned Captain James Cook recorded "Kodiak" in his journals fifteen years later in 1778. By 1784, Gregory Shelikof, another Russian explorer, set up a trading post on the island and began trading furs with the natives.

With Shelikof and his traders the story turned ugly. The Russians killed many of the native people and cowed the rest into indentured servitude. The trading post sent furs around the world and used the natives as slave labor. A Russian Orthodox Church mission, established in the 1790's added a Christian flavor to the settlement, but the harsh treatment of the natives continued. The performance emphasized the cultural and humanitarian aspects of the church's presence. The show's treatment of that time period did not exactly match the history books, presenting a positive slant on the story. In some ways it reminded me of the heroic tales of pioneers taming the western U. S. while ignoring the treatment of the native peoples.

We learned the Shelikof Company, which later merged into an organization called the Russia-America Company, established trading posts from Kodiak to Sitka, on the modern-day southeastern coast of Alaska. Alexander Baranov became the first governor of the area, appointed by the royal court in St. Petersburg, Russia. His influence and activities reached from Kodiak and Sitka to the Hawaiian islands where he traded goods with the natives,

Baranov also fought battles with the Tinglit peoples in and around Sitka and subdued them. Although he longed to return to Russia, communication with St. Petersburg was scarce and intermittent. While Baranov's wife and family remained in Russia, he took a native lover or slave and fathered several children. After learning of his wife's death, he married the lover and legitimized the children. His children then assumed roles in the company management, perpetuating their influence.

Baranov's replacement finally arrived in 1818 and he sailed for St. Petersburg via the Indian Ocean and Cape of Good Hope, but during a layover near Java in the then Dutch East Indies, he feel ill and died, never returning to Russia.

The storyline followed the basic outline of the Russian experience in Alaska, but ended with Baranov's death. The show gave no details of the U.S. purchase from Russia, nor the twentieth century development of the area. While entertaining and informative, we thought it went on a bit long.

After the performance we walked to the campground and settled in for the night. The campground was full of campers who came for the festival and show. A few revelers kept us awake until past midnight, but no rain or cloudy weather arrived. We slept well. After a breakfast in town consisting of sweet rolls and coffee, we viewed a few more booths and exhibits, then caught the minibus back to the airport.

We again gazed at the colossal Kodiak bear on display when we arrived to check in for our flight. Several small children stood near the bear while parents and grandparents, took photos. One child kept looking over his shoulder to see if the bear moved. Lucky for all of us he did not.

The weather for our flight back turned cloudy and gray. Clouds blocked most of the scenery as we again made a steep climb after takeoff, but the clouds cleared some over the ocean allowing us good views of Afognak Island and the Chugach mountains as we neared Anchorage.

The return flight experienced more turbulence than the flight out to Kodiak, but not so much as to make anyone ill. After a smooth landing and deplaning, the same young pilot thanked us again and wished us well. We drove over to Lake Spenard, a small lake near the airport, to grab some dinner and watch the float planes operating from the lake.

While we ate, several float planes, similar to the one we took to Kodiak Island, flew in, landed on the water, and taxied to a fuel station on the shore. Several planes also took off from the lake and the slow speeds obtained before liftoff amazed us. It fascinated us to watch the planes and try to guess when they would become airborne. The STOL planes always surprised us at the short distance needed and the slow speeds reached before lifting into the sky.

On Monday we told tales of our Kodiak excursion and found most of our crew had never been there although they touted it to us. We resisted any attempt to embellish the tale of seeing the mounted Kodiak bear at the airport. We only related it's huge size. The straight facts sufficed for that tall tale.

We soon had cause to wish we stayed on Kodiak island for another week.

# In the Land of the Midnight Sun

# Chapter 14
# Deal of a Lifetime

The next week on Sunday afternoon we drove along the Seward Highway, the main route south from town that makes up part of Alaska Route 1, when we began the most exciting and ultimately, frustrating experience of the summer.

We spent Saturday and Sunday working on the building lot for Richard's friend. Nothing fancy, just more clearing of trees and brush, and manual labor to help out. That weekend, we treated the McCulloch chainsaw with a lot more respect than our first experience. Saturday went without incident, but Sunday did not.

The building site sat along Rabbit Creek, just off Rabbit Creek Road about twelve miles south of town. That summer the area lay mostly undeveloped land, hence our efforts at clearing the building site. When I returned to the area in the summer of 2018, the entire area along Rabbit Creek Road had large homes situated on generous lots, worth over $1 million dollars each. In 1968 the best thing going for the area was potential.

On that Sunday afternoon the owner's wife joined us at the worksite. She and the owner sat outside the little travel trailer, drank coffee in the morning and beers in the afternoon, and watched us work. The owner occasionally pitched in with dragging limbs and brush into the large pile we created. For lunch, the lady provided egg salad sandwiches, potato chips, and a fruit salad. The owner offered us beer with the lunch, and we accepted.

Since our arrival in Anchorage, we bought beer from time to time, but always with an eye on our budget. This meant Schlitz and Ranier beer topped the list because the lowest prices went with them. I served as the main purchaser because I was over twenty-one, not because I was a beer connoisseur. At times, John bought some beer, usually when we traveled to small towns and areas away from the city where checking ID's seldom entered into the exercise. We went for whatever cost the least. This translated into poorer quality and taste in beers. We adjusted our tastes accordingly.

The sun shone that Sunday and the temperatures hit the high 60's Fahrenheit, a warm day for Anchorage. A beer sounded good to us because we had worked up a good sweat by lunchtime. The man handed us two cans of Budweiser, the "King of Beers" according to their advertising. I looked at John and he looked at me, both of us expecting a treat. After taking a good swig or two, we both offered the universal sign of a pleasing drink on a hot day, *"Ahhhh."* John looked at me and gave the thumbs up sign of his approval. Later, we discussed how those beers tasted so good we thought they might be champagne. Right there we resolved to save enough to buy a case of Budweiser and hoped it might last the rest of the summer.

We ate and talked about what places in Alaska we visited. The lady seemed impressed we used many weekends for travel in and around the area. She apologized for getting us to work that particular weekend, worried we missed another adventure. We expressed no reservations, saying we needed the money, especially now that we planned to buy better beer.

After half an hour we went back to work. The husband and wife walked the property checking the status of our work and the progress of the construction crews. At that point, a foundation and some framing was the extent of the work on the house. The man wore a pair of work boots and Levi's, the lady a pair of shorts and some slippers we called flip-flops. We paid little attention as they walked away from us.

## An Accident

Maybe an hour later, but probably less, the chainsaw roaring to John's direction and me stacking limbs into a pile, we saw the man running toward us. When the saw's roar died down, we heard the lady crying. She hopped on one foot several yards behind him with tears streaming down her face. Once we heard her sobbing, John dropped the saw and I dropped whatever I carried, and started toward them. Then we saw the problem.

A large nail jutted out the top of her left foot, extending a couple of inches above her instep. The flip-flop slipper remained stuck to her foot, this time more by the nail than the toehold. My stomach dropped as I stared at the foot and nail. She continued to sob and balance on her right foot. We saw little blood. The scary part was the nail coming out the top of her foot.

"Is it okay, if I take her to the emergency room?" The man addressed us with an excited voice.

"Of course!" We both seemed to answer at once.

He turned and put his arm around his wife's waist, offering support, as she hopped toward their car. She calmed some, maybe because she expected medical help or maybe because he supported her hobbling along. John ran to the car and opened the passenger side door just before they reached it. I stood helplessly to the side, wondering what else we might do for her.

The man hurried to take the wheel. Right before he slammed the door, he called to us, "Take the rest of the afternoon off, we'll settle up later." We just stood there watching the dust and gravel fly from the tires of the car as it left the property and joined the road.

After several seconds, John asked me, "Did he ask our permission to take her to the emergency?"

"Come to think of it, he did."

"That was strange." John added. "I wonder why he thought he needed our permission?"

"Maybe he got too excited and did not think clearly." I offered, but it did not make sense to me either.

We gathered the tools and locked them in the toolshed next to the little trailer. We picked up the beer cans and threw them in the back of the Pontiac. We talked about how scary her foot looked with the nail protruding and wondered why little blood flowed from it. The excitement of the accident stayed with us for a while until we realized it cost us about $6 in wages because we did not finish the afternoon. We did not dwell on it and decided to drive around town a bit.

Heading back toward downtown we remembered the swaying trees reminding the daughter of the earthquake, bringing on her panic attack, and now the wife suffering a nail through her foot. Maybe we brought bad luck with us.

We passed several businesses in the strip malls along the Seward Highway. At one red light as we waited, John pointed out a taxidermy and fur shop in the next block. Surprisingly, for a Sunday afternoon, it looked open with three people examining some furs and animal hides laid out on a table in front of the store. I agreed we should take a look, besides our afternoon was now open.

As we pulled into the parking lot, the others pulled away. We saw a young man, 17 or 18 years-old standing by the door to the shop. We nodded to him and walked over to the table.

I ran my hand over a wolf skin lying there. It felt smooth and soft to my touch. As my hand brushed across it, the hair ruffled a bit and then returned to its previous state, close to the hide. Next to the wolf skin was a large, white skin. I asked what it was.

"A polar bear skin." The young man replied as he walked toward me. John stood at the other end of the table looking at the various skins. I said something about how big the polar bear skin looked.

## The Fur and Taxidermy Shop

Remembering our experience telling our tale of the Great Alaskan Journey to other strangers, we launched into the story of how we ended up in Anchorage for the summer. The young man seemed more impressed with the Pontiac than he did with our journey, but he began talking to us.

He related how the shop belonged to his uncle who fell on tough times. We learned how the uncle planned to close the business and move back to the Lower 48 as quickly as he could. His wife received a cancer diagnosis and they needed to get back to Oregon for treatment. That meant a sale with big discounts on everything in the shop. The young man gestured toward the open door of the shop and stepped back from the table.

We talked several times over the summer about souvenirs or keepsakes from our summer in Alaska, but settled on nothing thus far. I wondered about the prices on some of the furs and skins, thinking I might try to buy a rug or something to take home. Earlier in a downtown fur shop we saw grizzly and polar bear rugs that fell far outside our price range, but the uncle's misfortune could be our good fortune. I had no idea what a mounted, bighorn ram's head cost but assumed it exceeded our budget.

We walked into the little shop to look around. The store remained fairly dark, none of the inside lights were lit. Looking toward the back of the shop I saw light coming through a broken window pane in the back door. Inside the walls held trophy heads of Bighorn and Dall Sheep. A huge stuffed grizzly bear stood in the corner behind another table. It was large, but nowhere near the size of a Kodiak bear. The skins and furs inside seemed poorly laid out for a sale, just heaped in a pile on two tables. I looked but saw no price tags on anything. John walked over and looked at the stuffed bear. The young man followed us inside.

"I can offer you a deal if something interests you. It is cash only, though." The young fellow walked behind the small counter in front of the mounted big horn ram's head. I asked about the polar bear skin on the table outside, expecting a response of several hundred dollars.

"Twenty dollars," came the reply. At that point John turned around and looked at me. He came over.

"What about the mounted bighorn ram?" I asked, my interest piqued.

"Twenty dollars." The same reply.

John elbowed me in the ribs and motioned toward the door. I followed him out front. We held a hushed discussion about the prices the young man mentioned, realizing they represented discounts far beyond anything we expected. We also compared notes on our cash on hand.

John spent lots of time in his dad's clothing and variety store and understood sales. They offered spring sales and fall sales when the different seasons dictated distinctive styles, but knew little about a going-out-of-busines sale. He surmised such an event might lead to a 50% discount, but he was not sure. He mentioned no one discounts things like this fellow unless they sorely needed money, and quickly. At Rose Auto, I knew Neal Rose might discount something 10% but rarely more unless he just wanted to get rid of it. Even as we discussed any misgivings, we thought about how we could take home something of real value as evidence of our trek north. The prices this fellow mentioned sounded too good to be true, but what did we know? Honestly, the true value of these furs, skins, and mounted heads escaped us, so we had no idea of the discount from fair value the man offered.

I went back to the table outside and pulled out the polar bear skin. I handed it to the young man and indicated I wanted to look some more. John followed suit with a wolfskin. The fellow took the items inside and piled them on the counter while we sorted through the other items out front.

A mahogany brown bear skin caught my eye. It measured about six feet long and four feet wide. The luxurious hide showed some dirt and debris, but felt soft to the touch. Some of the dust brushed away with my hand, making me think a professional cleaning might restore its natural sheen. I pulled it from the table and handed it to the young man.

Within a few minutes we accumulated two grizzly bear skins, two wolf skins, and the polar bear skin. If each cost $20, the total stood at $100 for the two of us. Turned out we had $120 cash on us. Our cash position might allow the addition of the big horn ram, fully mounted.

John and I returned to inside the shop and looked at the mounted head. We learned earlier that summer part of the trophy's stature and value came from the degree of curl in the horns. A big horn ram with what the trade called a 'full curl,' displayed a set of horns that extended and circled 360° from where it joined the skull. The trophy we looked at lacked a few degrees making the full curl, but exceeded anything we saw earlier. I looked at John and he nodded. We decided we wanted it although we did not discuss how we might get it home or how we might share it if we did.

We pointed toward the mounted head. The fellow took it down from the wall and laid it next to the other furs on the counter. John looked at me and I nodded, showing I thought we should try to add it to our purchases, even though it meant exhausting our cash. John agreed and pointed to the counter, showing we wanted it.

I fully expected to offer the $20 price we received earlier, totaling all the cash we had, but John just stood there not saying anything. After several seconds, the young man asked if we wanted all the stuff we laid out on the counter. John replied, "Maybe," and remained quiet. Another car pulled up.

We turned to look at the new arrivals and saw two men step out of a pickup. They approached the outside table which contained several wolf and bear skins. I thought about saying something, but remained quiet. The young man noticed the two men, but stayed with us.

"What if we take all of this?" John moved his hand over the pile which now included the bear skins, the wolf skins, the polar bear skin, and the mounted big horn.

"I think that is $120," came the reply.

John remained silent, just standing there. When it came to spending money, John often thought twice, or three times, before acting. He looked at me without making any hint of his thoughts. The young man looked at me then looked back at John. I remained quiet. Then, John turned his back on the man as if to leave.

I noticed the young man's hand shaking just a bit when he spoke up, "Okay, $100 cash, for all of it."

John smiled at me, turned, and told the man we would take it. We reached into our billfolds, and each pulled out $50, splitting it down the middle. I knew John well enough, and knew he felt the same about me, that we would divide up the total purchase without any hassle or hurt feelings. I remember thinking, *"Where on earth could I put that big horn ram?"*

We loaded everything in the trunk except the mounted big horn. We put it in the back seat as if it were a passenger. The wolf skins, grizzly bear skins, and polar bear skin filled the trunk. We drove back to the apartment, removed everything from the car and laid them out on the floor of the main room. Wendy saw us unloading and came over to see our prizes. We did not tell her the price, just that we got a great deal because the owner needed to move to Oregon. Wendy grinned and suggested lying on the polar bear skin would feel good on one's bare skin. No one accepted her offer.

Charlie with wolf skins, bear skins and Big Horn Ram

Later, we tacked the two wolf skins, and a bear skin to the wall behind the refrigerator. We placed the big horn atop the refrigerator and pushed a coffee can filled with sand against it for support. It looked as if it belonged against that wall. I draped the polar bear skin over the refrigerator and held up the other bear skin while John took a photo. Too bad we had no flash because the photo turned out poorly.

We went to bed that night thinking about our purchases, completely forgetting the poor lady with the nail through her foot. We could not wait to tell the work crew about our good fortune. Maybe one of them would want to stop by the shop and pick up a bargain bear skin.

Next morning, we did not wait for the break to announce our good luck. John told of seeing the fur and taxidermy shop along the highway and mentioned the general address. I jumped in and mentioned the huge polar bear skin. Everyone on the work crew seemed to share our enthusiasm and we continued talking until Gabriele told us it was time to work. At break, we picked up the conversation and told about the other skins and the mounted big horn. We did not mention the price paid, only that we got a tremendous bargain due to the owner's bad luck. Joe and Paul both asked for specific directions to the shop. We asked for recommendations of a place to get the skins cleaned or evaluated. Each man mentioned a different professional fur cleaning shop which led to an argument about prices, skills, and professionalism of the two shops. We got the addresses and paid little attention to the rest of their dispute.

After work we needed to do our grocery shopping and took no action on seeking out a fur cleaning shop. We enjoyed looking at our prizes and acted like big game hunters even though we had no part in securing the trophies. We resolved to follow up on Tuesday.

Work went well and the crew asked more questions about our purchases. We took some pride in talking about the wolf skins and the bear skins, but especially liked describing the mounted big horn. I regaled them with a description of its almost full curl to the horns. Joe mentioned he stopped by the shop Monday evening and found it closed, all locked up.

After work we took the skins to one of the shops Joe and Paul recommended. It looked respectable with a large sales room. It had fur coats, gloves, hats, and fancy items made from fur, all looking great and for sale at prices much higher than we paid for our haul. The principal who dealt with the cleaning and processing of skins was away, only a salesman staffed the shop. He asked for John's driver's license, took the furs, carefully preparing a receipt with a description for each one, and told us to check back on Friday or Saturday. The shop's expert would quote us a price for cleaning all the items. We left the wolf skins and bear skins and pocketed the receipt. The mounted big horn remained on top of our refrigerator.

We discussed each taking home a wolf skin and a bear skin. That left the polar bear skin and the big horn. We talked about having the polar bear skin made into a rug and who might have a place for the big horn. We left the ultimate decision for later, figuring we could make that decision when we headed home.

Friday could not come soon enough. We wanted to know the price for cleaning the skins and the price of making the polar bear skin into a rug. We hurried home from work to change clothes and clean up a bit before we headed to the fur cleaning shop.

I put on a clean shirt and John was washing up in the bathroom when I heard a knock on the door. I thought, *"Oh great, what does Wendy want now,"* and went to the door. I opened the door with a speech already prepared to tell Wendy we needed to leave right away and would catch up with her later. I never got to give the speech.

## The Alaska State Trooper

A tall, sun-glass-wearing, Alaska State Trooper, complete with his Smokey the Bear hat and Colt .45 strapped to his waist, stood in front of me.

"Hello," was all I could think to say.

"Mr. St. Clair?'

"No, but he is here." I responded wondering what was up. My mind raced, *"Had we received any parking or speeding tickets and why would a state trooper respond for something like that?"*

John stepped into the main room, ready to go downtown. His face took on a puzzled look.

The trooper asked if he could come in, he wanted to talk to us about something. I motioned for him to come in as Wendy appeared in the doorway as if to see what the trooper was doing there. I held up my hand as if to let Wendy know we were busy, and shut the door.

John pulled a chair from the kitchen table for the trooper and we sat down on the couch.

"I got your name and this address from the fur cleaning shop downtown." He began addressing his business with us. John and I looked at each other still confused about his visit.

The trooper hesitated while he looked directly at the big horn atop the refrigerator. He turned back toward us and resumed talking.

The story he told took the wind from our sails. It seemed the young man we met at the fur and taxidermy shop was a disgruntled employee who broke into the shop on Sunday afternoon and proceeded to sell assorted items from the shop without any permission from the owner. The owner found the shop in disarray on Monday morning, reported several items missing, and surmised his employee might be the culprit. The authorities quickly found and arrested the young man. He remained in jail awaiting further charges.

The tale included a description of two men who spoke with southern accents and drove a late model Pontiac. The thief described us pretty well, but the decisive factor was the alert given to the other fur dealers in town. That led to our wolf skins and bear skins at the shop for evaluation and a detailed receipt with a name and address. Of course, the police considered our furs stolen property destined for return to owner.

The trooper asked about our interaction with the young man on Sunday. He patiently heard our side of the story before continuing. He asked several questions about if we knew the young man, had we dealt with him before, did we understand how valuable the skins were, and could we give him the name of our supervisor at work. It dawned on us he thought we might be complicit in the breaking and entering and the thefts. He took several pages of notes in his notebook. We confessed everything and mentioned more than once the $100 we paid for the stuff.

He reviewed his notes, looked at the big horn again, and then spoke to us. It went something like the following.

"If you return everything, including the ram's head over the refrigerator, I will recommend no charges against you. It appeared to you the fellow had authority to sell the items, even though the prices were ridiculously low. It also seems to be you had nothing to do with the break-in." We heard and appreciated his assessment.

"But, what about our $100?" We seemed to ask at the same time.

"I am afraid I cannot help you with that." He continued that we could pursue a claim against the thief, but the authorities would not help with it.

At that time, we knew only a few weeks remained on our adventure, not enough for a small claims action against the thief.

It dawned on us deciding who got the polar bear rug and who got the big horn just became moot.

The trooper took his notebook, his sun glasses, his sidearm, his trooper hat, and our big horn ram's head with the almost full curl, and left. He mentioned if he needed anything else he would be in touch. Our elation from Sunday afternoon had lasted less than five days.

Wendy returned to our door step a few minutes after the trooper left and became the first to hear our tale of woe. Mostly, she remarked on how cute she thought the trooper was. She expressed no sorrow at the $100 we lost.

Later that night, John asked if we should call Lem and see if he would loan us $100. We laughed at our predicament, but only for a minute. Thank goodness Friday was pay day, and the $100, while a big loss, would not break us.

The most awkward thing we faced came with our explanations to the work crew. On Monday they wanted to know what we learned about our furs, and we told the tale, complete with the trooper removing the big horn from the top of our refrigerator. At first, they seemed sympathetic, but by afternoon break a universal theme appeared: *"How could you be so stupid? Dumb tenderfeet."*

Upon reflection, we agreed.

Years later, John and I talked about our adventure several times and we always included the visit by the Alaska State Trooper. Life's lesson learned: *If it appears too good to be true, it is.*

# Chapter 15
# King

One day at lunch break I went outside for a little sunshine. My thoughts bounced around between how great the freshly waxed and buffed school room floor looked, and the demonstrations at the Democratic Party's National Convention in Chicago. It was Thursday, the last week of August.

We planned to work until the end of the month which meant our last work day came Friday, August 30, also payday. That left the Labor Day weekend for us to do more exploring. A week later, Friday, September 6, we planned to fly home. That left us a few days to get things together, sell the Pontiac, and arrange for a ride to the airport. We packed a lot of adventures into the past twelve weeks, but wanted to add a few more.

While justifiably proud of the beautiful job we did on the floor, the long-range benefit of my work escaped me. We stripped the floor of each classroom and hallway, completely removing the old build-up of wax from previous years. Then we mopped the floors as clean as possible when you use a mop squeezed repeatedly in the same bucket. The first two or three dunks and squeezes left the water fairly clean, but after ten or twelve such dunkings, the water looked a little cloudy. After the mopping, we put down a generous coat of wax and then buffed the entire floor to a glossy shine. Looking down a hallway with the gleaming, newly waxed floor, made us proud. The classrooms looked great too before we returned the desks and chairs, which hid 80% of our excellent work. My thinking took me to what happens the first day of school? Each hallway and classroom would be spic and span clean with a glossy, freshly waxed floor. Then two hundred plus youngsters would enter the school and obliterate our efforts within minutes. Regardless of the ultimate outcome, we received our $2.42 per hour and followed Gabriele's directions.

## Unrest in Chicago

We listened to the morning and evening radio news reporting on the violent demonstrations in Chicago. By this time, I adjusted to the idea Lyndon Johnson would not stand for re-election, but had mixed feelings about who the democrats might nominate. At that time, I began to doubt the efficacy of America's role in the Vietnam war. Hubert Humphrey looked to become Johnson's successor, but many young demonstrators loudly protested the war and wanted Eugene McCarthy, the peace candidate. Emotions ran high and raw after the assassinations of Martin Luther King, Jr., and Robert F. Kennedy and many protestors pushed the bounds of civil disobedience.

Chicago's mayor, Richard J. Daley, wanted no protests and severely restricted access, areas for demonstrations, and permits for parades. The Chicago police made thinly veiled threats about beating any protesters, and many young people came to town looking for a confrontation. It came on Wednesday evening, August 28, and the Chicago police arrested many demonstrators. One of those was Jerry Rubin, who I saw two years earlier protesting at the House Un-American Activities Committee hearings. My experiences in Washington D. C. led me to keep up more with politics than I ever did before, and the problems at the convention in Chicago led the news each hour.

While my thoughts drifted, I saw a white flash through the bushes at the edge of the school ground. It looked like a tassel one might find on a ski cap, a white ball that bounced up and down and back and forth. Soon I saw a man with a husky dog come walking out of the bushes and onto the playground. The white tassel was clearly the plume-like end of the dog's curved tail, which stood high over his back and rear. I walked over to see the dog.

"Is he an Alaskan husky?" I inquired of the man even though I thought I recognized the type of dog. The dog appeared well trained and friendly. He had a thick coat, even for August, broad shoulders, and a stocky build. His face exhibited the trademark, husky mask over the eyes and snout.

"No, he's a Malamute."

He let me pet the dog. I rubbed his head between the ears, and he enjoyed it. He did not bark, but kept looking at the man as if awaiting instructions. We talked more and I asked how a Malamute differed from a Siberian Husky. The man knew quite a bit about the dogs and told me they had similar traits and appearances, but if you looked closely, you could tell the difference. The main difference was eye color. The Siberian Husky often had piercing blue eyes, while the Malamutes always had dark, brown eyes. He told me both were friendly with people, had a double coat to protect against the winter cold, had high energy, and needed a strong owner they respected. He continued by saying some of the differences came in their interaction with humans: the Malamutes enjoyed being around humans, the Siberian Huskies much more aloof. He pointed to the dog's shoulders and said the Malamutes were bigger, heavier, and carried broader shoulders, and the Huskies were lighter, faster dogs. Both made great sled pulling dogs; the Malamutes had more endurance, but the Huskies could run faster, just not as far. The dog and the man's knowledge of the breeds impressed me.

My girlfriend-fiancé owned a German Shepherd and liked bigger dogs. I wondered about having a dog of my own and liked the looks of the Malamute. My impression of the dog started ideas of getting a dog to take home.

That summer both John and I read the Jack London novels, Call of the Wild and White Fang, both stories about a dog and a wild wolfdog with adventures in the far north. We liked the settings in the wild country of the Yukon and Alaska and the way London spun tales interweaving men, the wild outdoors, and how both domesticated and wild animals relate to humans. Reading the stories made me wonder how I might relate to a wild dog or wolfdog. The Malamute might not completely fit the bill, but it came close.

I asked how one went about getting a dog like that.

He responded that this dog could be available if I had an interest. The man related how he needed to move to Fairbanks the next week to work with other sled dogs. He owned two other dogs and did not have room for this dog. I asked his name. He answered, "Tony." I was too embarrassed to say I meant the dog, not him, and answered, "I am Charlie, and the dog's name?"

"King."

My mind flashed to the popular television show, "Sergeant Preston of the Yukon." It was on the air for a few years during the mid-1950's when John and I attended elementary school. I thought of Sergeant Preston's dog, King, as I remembered it. Later, John reminded me the dog's name, in the show was Yukon King. At any rate, I remembered the dog in the show looked a lot like this King and thought the name appropriate.

As a kid, I loved the show and its sponsor, Quaker Oats, so much that I urged my mother to buy boxes and boxes of Quaker's Puffed Wheat and Puffed Rice in an effort to secure a genuine deed to one square inch of a lot in the Yukon Territory. The show advertised a way to own part of the Yukon with a deed issued from the Klondike Big Inch Land Co. Inc., and the ad proved successful, at least to this viewer. I never received a box of cereal with the deed and became disillusioned years later when I learned land around Ashcroft, Colorado, served as the Yukon scenes in the show.

The story developed around Sergeant Preston, a Royal Canadian Mounted Policeman working in the Yukon Territory. He finds a Malamute puppy who became separated from its mother and raised by a wolf. When the wolf tangled with a cougar and lost, Sergeant Preston rescues the puppy and raises him along with his sled dog team. Through several episodes, King proved his mettle by heroically rescuing or saving the Mountie from all sorts of trouble. My memories of the show made this dog, King, that much more intriguing.

The exotic land portrayed in the television series and the heroic deeds Sergeant Preston and his dog achieved, added to the mystique of Alaska and the Yukon and my desire to visit. Whatever pushed the idea in my mind, it came about that summer.

I asked if he lived near the school and might be around on Friday. He pointed to a house across the street and said he would be there until Wednesday of next week. I told him our crew needed another day to finish the school and I might contact him again.

That afternoon on break I went to the library in the school and looked for a book on husky dogs. I learned the Alaskan Malamute ranked among the oldest of the sled dog breeds in the Arctic regions. One book indicated they came from domesticated wolfdogs who may have accompanied the Paleolithic hunters across the land bridges of the Bering Strait 4,000 years ago. The Inuit peoples developed the dogs as sled pullers of heavy loads at low speeds over long distances. Some described the Malamutes as freighters, and the Siberian Husky, bred across the ocean in Russia and trained for lighter loads at faster speeds, as racers.

All the books described the dogs as energetic, friendly with humans, and loyal. I thought those traits made for a good pet.

## Getting a Dog

That night I discussed the possibility of getting the dog with John and he expressed misgivings. He worried how a dog raised in the far north might manage the heat and humidity of central Texas. We talked about the planning of getting a dog from Anchorage to Waco, Texas where my studies at Baylor University resumed in only a couple of weeks. I agreed the idea of taking a dog home might stretch my budget and present lots of logistical challenges. Based on my story of what a good-looking dog King was, John did agree to take a look at the dog on Friday.

Nearing the end of August and dreading the long drive back to Texas, we had discussed selling the Pontiac and flying home. We settled on that strategy the week before. If we thought the dog could safely make the trip, a travel crate and discounted airfare could seal the deal.

In the mid to late 1960's airlines promoted what they called a "Student Standby Fare," at half the price of the standard fare. Many airlines in those days flew at less than capacity which made seats available and the fare very attractive. The airlines figured any fare counted more than an empty seat. The main problem came when all seats went to passengers paying full fare. Then the student lost the seat or 'got bumped' to the next available flight to his destination. This required some flexibility for scheduling, but many students took advantage of it. We never tried it before, but even with the uncertainty of a non-guaranteed seat, we figured it beat a week in the car headed south. Neither of us wanted to endure those long days in the Pontiac if we could avoid it.

The marketing folks at the airlines figured in addition to bringing in any revenue from what would otherwise be empty seats, the Student Standby Fares might create demand from a whole generation hooked on flying. If a student liked the experience on a particular airline, using that airline became more likely once the student reached age 22.

On Friday during our lunch break John and I walked over to the dog owner's residence to inquire about the Malamute. He welcomed us and took us to the backyard where three husky looking dogs got up to greet us. The Malamute was the biggest and oldest of the group. My imagination or vanity led me to believe the dog remembered me from the day before. John agreed King was a fine-looking dog.

We talked about the dog's availability and at what price. The fellow mentioned $20, which made me think of the young man at the fur and taxidermy shop where everything appeared to cost $20. The owner said the dog should adjust to the warmer climate, mentioning that it carried a double coat of fur which thickened during the winter months, and in warmer temperatures, the coat would not grow as thick. He thought it might take a full winter before the dog's fur fully adjusted, but it should not hurt the animal's health. Without much more than this conjecture, I decided on the spot to take a chance and told him I wanted the dog. We made arrangements for me to pick up the dog after work and pay him. The idea of owning a real, live, Alaskan Malamute excited me.

John kept some of his misgivings, but did not protest. He mentioned at least we did not have much more time in Anchorage to look after a dog.

Instead of working until 4:30 p.m. that Friday, Gabriele called the work crew together at 4. She and the ladies arranged a farewell party for us, complete with cake and punch. The party surprised us although all week we talked to each crew member about things we learned from them and how we enjoyed working on the crew. Each seemed impressed we took the summer off from college studies to come all the way to Alaska. John and I were proud of the summer, too, but knew it was a means to an end, not a career or job for the rest of our lives. That reflection made us a little sad for the crew members, but excited about getting on with our lives. Gabriele praised our work ethic and wished us well as we headed to Texas.

After the party, we shook hands with the men, hugged the women, and said our goodbyes. We thanked the ladies for the party, helped clean up the plates and napkins, and took the rest of the cake. Our parting from the crew we came to like was bittersweet. Bitter in that our relationship with the people was ending and we would never see them again, and sweet because we came to like them and knew they liked us.

We walked over to the dog owner's residence and picked up King. He acted excited to see us. The owner on the other hand, looked at little sad. As he brought the dog around to the car, he knelt down and gave King a big hug, then rubbed his head. The owner gave me a short rope with a latch on the end to hook to King's collar and warned me he could be headstrong at times. King jumped right in the back seat of the car and sat up looking first at me, then at John.

Back at the apartment I put down some towels and an old blanket for a dog bed. We used a small saucer for a water bowl. I took King for a walk while John went to the supermarket to buy some canned dog food. We only got a few yards from the apartment before I understood what the man meant about King's headstrong nature. King pulled me with him as we walked into a stand of pine trees. Other than stopping to pee every few yards, he pulled hard against the rope in my hand as we walked. I finally wrapped the rope around my wrist, fearing he might pull the rope right out of my hand and take off. I decided to pull back, hard; trying to assert

King, an Alaskan Malamute

myself as the dominant one. King's actions mimicked mine, trying to assert himself. We walked for half an hour and found John at the apartment when we returned.

Wendy saw me and King return and came over. She wanted to know about the dog and did we plan to take it to Texas. King seemed friendly around her also, making me think he must like humans in general. She offered to go with me on a walk with King, but I begged off by saying we just completed a long walk. I tried to deter her from asking about other walks by saying I needed to have King's undivided attention until he grew acquainted with me. She did not protest, rubbed his ears again, and returned to her apartment.

That weekend we took King on a hike close to Rabbit Creek Road and Turnagain Arm where we worked on the building site. Each time we started to walk, King tried to assert himself and forced me to tug hard on his leash. After we walked a bit, he let up some, but I always wondered when he might try to pull away from me.

We got into some fairly mushy ground looking for a lake we saw on the map. Our boots sank into the watery ground as we pushed through some alder brushes looking for the small lake. All of a sudden, King stopped and raised his head high, his ears pointing skyward. He did not bark, so I wondered what got his attention. He stood as if frozen in place. I took a couple of steps coming to his side. He kept the same rigid posture and looked straight ahead. Following his gaze, I saw it. A large, cow moose stood about thirty feet away, chomping on some leaves. King remained quiet while John walked up to see why we stopped. The moose either did not see us or remained unconcerned. She continued to put her head up to a branch and use her teeth to strip off the leaves in a quick movement down the branch, catching the leaves in her mouth.

John asked in a whisper if we saw a calf with her, mentioning an offspring born in May or June could accompany her. If so, we needed to be careful and not spook her. We read about how hostile a mother moose could get if she, or the baby, became threatened. The last thing we needed right then with our feet in boggy ground, was an 800-pound irate animal charging us. To our surprise, King stayed quiet.

We backed slowly away from the moose, trying to be quiet, still not seeing a calf. When we doubled the space between us and the moose, we saw the calf wander over to the cow. The calf stood about waist high to us and as ungainly as anything we could remember.

John asked me if I knew what a moose looked like. I made a face at him and pointed toward the cow and calf. He smiled and answered, "A moose looks like a horse created by committee." Seeing the gangling calf, I agreed.

We continued to backtrack and when we reached some distance from the moose, John asked why King did not bark. I did not have an answer, but expressed my appreciation for his silence. A barking dog would have brought us to the attention of mama moose, and who knew what might happen next.

We made a big circle around the moose and calf and made our way to the edge of the little lake. John pulled out his fishing rod while King and I explored the area some more. Each time King and I went for a walk we repeated the drill about who was in charge, but his rebellious streak lasted a shorter and shorter period each time. I decided we gained some familiarity with each other, and he began to accept me as his leader. I asked him why he did not bark at the moose, but he didn't answer.

The days that followed allowed us to get better acquainted with King. Everyone who met him agreed he was a fine specimen. He allowed everyone to pet him, usually rubbing his ears or patting his broad shoulders. Not everyone agreed King would like the Texas heat. I wondered about that too, but remained committed to finding out.

Each morning and evening King and I took walks. He loved it and always looked excited when I grabbed the rope and leash. True to his breeding, his stamina lasted longer than mine on our walks. He showed no signs of fatigue, but I usually wanted to go rest after half an hour. It pleased me that he showed less orneriness and assertiveness as we continued our routine.

I checked with United Airlines about renting a crate and King's fare to Denver. The route home took both John and me through Seattle, then me on to Denver and John on to Dallas. The airline warned me that my student fare came subject to bumping if the plane filled with full fare passengers, but King would go from Seattle to Denver on the next flight, whether I made it or not. I called Hungie and alerted her to our schedule and that an Alaskan Malamute was coming. The idea of meeting King at the airport in Denver excited her, but she expressed a desire that we come at the same time. I agreed to call from Seattle if I missed the flight to Denver.

As it turned out, King took the direct route and I got stuck in Seattle, but more on that later. King did well in Texas, living for a while in Waco before settling in as my daddy's best friend in Morton. King and the Judge spent many an hour walking up to the high school and circling the running track. They became a familiar sight around our hometown as every evening when daddy returned home, King excitedly jumped and ran around until they started on their walks. Daddy remarked how King pushed him to keep up the exercise regimen. Some nights when daddy came home late and tired, King was still excited to go for a walks, and his importunity led daddy to relent and go with him, at times after 10 p.m. King lived another several years to the end of his life with my daddy. They were both good for each other.

King also gained the reputation of one tough dog. Despite his good nature around people, he did not get along well with other dogs. Daddy related a couple of scrapes King had with other, sometimes bigger dogs, and usually sent the big dogs running home with their tails between their legs, thoroughly chastened for taking him on in a tussle. His loyalty made him protective of daddy and quick to defend his territory.

One Christmas Hungie and I took King to Ruidoso where he reveled in the snow. King loved the snow and cold temperatures. He stretched out his front legs and rubbed his belly against the snow as though he missed the north country. It made me wonder about bringing him to Texas, and whether, somehow, he missed Alaska. I decided King's companionship with my daddy made taking that risk worthwhile.

For all the days King lived after Anchorage, no one ever reported hearing him bark. Maybe Malamute includes mute in the name because the dogs do not bark. Overall, King turned out to be a devoted, but almost silent friend. He and daddy, the Judge, got along well for many people said my daddy was also a man of few words.

# In the Land of the Midnight Sun

# Chapter 16
# Heading Home

Leaving our jobs at the end of August gave us a week plus the Labor Day weekend to prepare for the journey home. We had to find a buyer for the car, pack, and arrange a ride to the airport for two Texans and an Alaskan dog.

Once John decided to sell the car, we checked with Richard about options. He recommended that we go to the General Motors dealer in Anchorage where they sold Chevys, Pontiacs, Oldsmobiles, Buicks, Cadillacs, and GM trucks. Richard thought the dealer would treat us better than a used car lot. We gave that task priority because we did not know how long it might take, in that John was one slow to make up his mind, especially where money was involved, and we knew he might want to sleep on an offer before deciding.

On Tuesday morning after taking King for a good walk and finishing breakfast, we mapped out the GM dealership and drove there to see what they might offer for the Pontiac. We had misgivings about selling the car since it shared so many memories with us that summer, but neither of us savored the idea of driving it back to Texas. It proved itself to us, but familiarity and fond memories only went so far.

John informed the reception lady he wanted to sell a car and she introduced him to the used car manager. A fifty-something year-old man with a short-sleeved shirt, long skinny tie, and male pattern baldness came over to greet us. I let John do all the talking. Beforehand, we discussed whether Alaskan used car salesmen enjoyed a better reputation than those in Texas and agreed they were much the same. Whatever car selling and buying experience that person had before meeting John, he needed more.

## Selling the Pontiac

After learning of our situation and the reason John wanted to sell the car, the manager asked to drive it. We waited while he took the car for a test drive and then another half an hour while the car sat in the mechanic's bay for even more inspection. Finally, the used car manager called us in to talk. We joined him in a little room, not really an office, off the service area of the dealership. He complimented John on the car's condition and appearance and then spent several minutes telling John why the Pontiac was not worth the same in Anchorage as it might be in Texas. We looked at each other figuring he knew we wanted to fly instead of drive home, and therefore were eager to sell, but we said nothing.

John remained quiet while the man talked about the car's demerits. It only had two doors, instead of four. Its tan color was not a popular one in Alaska. The tires, while serviceable, would need replacing before a sale. The V-8 engine required more gasoline and gas in Alaska was expensive. Most Alaskans wanted something with 4-wheel drive and more storage room. His list of deficiencies seemed endless. John just sat there waiting for the money discussion.

Finally, the used car manager mentioned a low-ball amount he would recommend to the general manager of the dealership.

He continued that the offer would not be effective until he got approval, but he would sure try. Unbeknownst to the used car man, those two statements told John quite a lot about the negotiation. First, the fellow thought he had a rookie or someone badly wanting to sell, hence the low-ball offer. Second, the man did not have the authority to make the deal. I was surprised when John stood up without saying anything. I quickly joined him.

"Well, thanks for your time." John spoke as a courtesy, turned, and reached for the door to the little room.

Then turning to me, John said, "Looks like we have a good drive ahead of us."

Before I could join John in the doorway, the man spoke up, "Well, let me see if I can get approval for a little more. It will only take a minute."

John, without stepping back into the room, asked "How much is a little more?"

"$250."

"No thanks." John turned and stepped further away from the room and the man. I came alongside him while the man followed us into the hallway.

"Okay, let me see if I can get approval for $350 more."

John stopped but did not say anything. The man looked at me and I in turn, looked at John.

"Okay, see what you can do," John answered, and we returned to the room.

John watched as the man exited the service area and walked across the salesroom floor to a large, corner office with a sign designating the manager for the entire dealership. John took note of the dealership manager. We could see the men talking, but could not hear the exchange. After less than a minute, the used car man returned.

"Good news, I got approval for $250 above my first recommendation."

John's face showed no emotion while he asked, "What happened to the $350?"

"I could not get that approved."

John stood up and I followed. As we exited, John mentioned how we needed to check with other dealers, but we might be back. I said nothing, but noticed John did not reach to shake the man's hand.

Instead of going to check with others about the car, we drove downtown for lunch. We both ordered cheeseburgers instead of the daily feature, salmon fillet on a bed of rice. We both felt we had eaten enough salmon for the summer.

I needed some souvenirs/gifts to take home to my family. Since our great fur and taxidermy fiasco, I looked only at reputable dealers with established retail outlets. The downtown area hosted most of them. I looked at some gloves, hats, and a couple of stoles my mother could wrap around her shoulders. I settled on a lined, seal skin hat with ear flaps for daddy. I thought he could wear it to a football game some November Friday night when the weather turned cold.

L-R Men's and Women's Seal Fur Hats, purchased in Alaska, 1968

For my mother I found a seal skin, pillbox style hat that looked fashionable to me. I liked its looks although I was not sure where she might wear it. The hats totaled $30.

For my sisters, I decided on some small, oil paintings of the Northern Lights above a mountain landscape. Even though we did not see the Aurora Borealis, we saw lots of photographs and paintings featuring the natural phenomena. The small paintings definitely represented Alaska and were affordable.

Earlier I asked a tradesman to make two pair of Mukluks; high, soft boots, made from Caribou skins instead of the traditional seal skins. I had bought a Caribou hide at a fair and thought Mukluks fashioned from the hide would look great. The tradesman did not talk me out of my idea. I had one pair for Hungie and one pair for me. I envisioned us using them in the snows of Colorado. We kept them for a few years, but I learned my mistake. The Caribou skins shed their fur easily and did not retain the warmth and water resistance of seal skins. The Caribou skins came at a much lower price than seal skins and I came to understand why. After a few years in the closet, I threw them away in the 1970's.

We spent the rest of the day shopping for trinkets and souvenirs for our families. Things fell into two categories: touristy junk or high-end furs. We focused on the touristy junk. We had a great afternoon walking up and down 3rd, 4th, and 5th Streets in downtown Anchorage. Along the way I asked John about the car.

"My dad said one of the best negotiating tactics is the willingness to walk away. I thought the guy low-balled me and I wanted him to know nothing required me to take the deal. We might go back on Thursday and see."

## Making a Deal

John also mentioned next time he would ask for the owner-manager, not the used car manager. He said that was another thing he learned from his dad, always deal with the decision maker. John's dad died two years before while I was in Washington D.C., and it became clear to me over the summer, he continued to grieve his loss. We talked about it a few times and I believe, it brought us closer. Luckily, my daddy lived another twenty-one years, but I often thought about my experience with John that summer and wondered how I would manage such a loss. When my daddy died, my experience confirmed what John and I talked about that summer. Grief comes and goes. You cannot set a schedule to it. It happens on its own time. I think both John and I matured that summer as we celebrated the good, strong relationships each of us had with our fathers.

John later told me that summer prodded him to grow up and welcome the responsibilities of adulthood. As the youngest in a family of four children, John enjoyed many of the advantages common to a youngest child, but his experiences that summer allowed him to step away from the carefree days of a teen. Besides being a good friend and companion for me that summer, those months helped John as he grew into a mature and responsible adult.

Although I had no financial gain coming from the sale of John's car, I wanted to sell it, mostly to avoid driving it back to Texas. Even though the delay made me a little anxious, knowing John was channeling his dad's advice and experience, made me feel confident in his ability to get a good deal for the Pontiac. I was right.

We returned to the dealership on Thursday afternoon and true to form, John asked for the owner. After the receptionist heard our request and relayed it to the owner, a well-dressed man in his sixties' greeted us and welcomed us to his corner office. He wore a white, long-sleeved shirt and a narrow, dark blue tie with the Alaska State emblem — The Big Dipper Constellation and Polaris, embroidered in gold. He looked and acted in a professional manner.

Upon learning this was our second visit to his company, he called the used car salesman on the inner-office phone. We listened to only one side of the conversation, but could tell he received the information on the Pontiac and the used car manager's assessment. We noted he did not invite the man to join us.

John's 1967 Pontiac on 4th Street across from the Anchorage Westward Hotel
No, that is not the Chuck Wagon in the background, although it could be its twin.

The owner picked up with the last offer, $250 over the low-ball opening bid from the used car manager. John waited several seconds before saying anything.

"It is only a year old, had one owner, and has low mileage." John ignored the dollar amount, implying his rejection of it by talking about the car's strong points.

The owner looked at John with a barely perceptible smile. It occurred to me he enjoyed the interaction. Half a minute passed without anyone saying anything while I wondered what might happen next. John told me earlier part of his dad's advice included remaining silent during the bargaining, adding that often the first one to speak loses. The owner broke the silence by offering to raise his price by $100 to $350, the used car manager's highest suggestion. John looked at me, but I could not tell what he thought. He hesitated before answering as if he seriously considered the last offer. After what I considered a long pause, he added, "I would like to sell the car. If you could raise that to $500, we have a deal."

Now it was the owner's time to remain silent. He just sat there without an expression. John said no more. I watched both of them for what seemed like a full minute of more silence. They looked intently at each other with no discernible expressions.

The owner raised his bid to $400 on top of the low-ball bid. John squinted his eyes just a bit and frowned ever so slightly, but said nothing. The owner looked intently at John while I expected John to confirm the deal. Instead, John said, "I hate for $100 to keep us from a deal. It is a good car and in good condition."

The owner appeared to just sit still, not smiling or frowning. Then it surprised me to see a slight grin on his face and hear his next word.

"Done." The owner took John's offer. This added another $500 above the original offer to John's pocket bringing the total to $2,000, two-thirds of the original purchase price eighteen months and a long drive to Alaska after the initial purchase. I experienced a tuition-free seminar in salesmanship and bargaining watching these two men work out a deal.

The owner directed his finance man to draw a cashier's check while John signed over the title to the car. The owner shook our hands and wished us luck. Before we left, he asked if we enjoyed our summer in Alaska. We both answered at the same time, "Yes sir, we did."

After catching a cab to the bank to cash the check and then to our apartment, we rehashed the deal. I expressed my admiration at John's bargaining skills and his cool head under the pressure of selling the Pontiac or driving it back to Texas. John poo-pooed his skills, but did say sometimes it is good to remain quiet. He was pleased with the sale, and I felt good for him.

Earlier, we arranged our co-worker Joe to pick us up on Friday afternoon and take us to the airport. Our last night in the apartment found us cleaning and mopping the floor. We had no wax or buffer, but thought it looked better than we found it, and best of all, due to our distribution to the neighbors, the freezer compartment held no salmon. The apartment manager came by Friday, inspected the place, and returned our deposit. Our last duty was to close and lock the door as we left. The apartment served us well over the summer, and our closest neighbors were nice and friendly, or in Wendy's case, a little too friendly.

Joe took us to the airport around 5 p.m. which gave us plenty of time to catch the 10 p.m. flight to Seattle. We loaded King into a crate at the baggage area and included Hungie's name and phone number in Denver, in case he arrived before me. Then we treated Joe to dinner.

We splurged by ordering King Crab, even though we knew airport food prices offered no bargain. Joe seemed pleased and we enjoyed ourselves reminiscing about the summer, our work crew, and the good times. Joe mentioned how we saw and experienced more of Alaska in one summer than he had in the past five years. We agreed with him, we had seen a lot and we had experienced one event-filled summer. Joe also informed us Dutch Harbor was in the Aleutian Islands and Yakutat was in the southeast of Alaska near Glacier Bay.

Photo: Google Earth

Our overnight flight to Seattle left at 10 p.m. for the five-hour flight. Despite the darkness and the long flight, neither of us slept much. Given the time change we arrived in Seattle at 5 a.m. to find the airport deserted.

In an hour, the coffee shop opened and by 7 a.m. things picked up considerably. John's flight to Dallas included plenty of seats for a Student Standby Fare and he departed at 9:30. We shook hands and hugged, both of us sporting ear-to-ear grins as he walked down the jetway. It felt like the end of a remarkable story, one cemented by good friendship and compatible personalities. John proved one great traveling companion through thick and thin. Now, I needed to get to Denver.

## Stuck in Seattle

I hustled over to the gate for my 10:30 a.m. United Airlines flight to Denver. Now that John was on his way to Texas, I wanted to get moving. After a long time in the line to the gateway desk, the attendant shook her head when she saw my fare. She checked a couple of things on her desk, then looked at another booklet before turning to me and informing me the flight was full. She recommended that I wait to confirm everyone checked in, but it did not look good. Her prediction proved out. After the plane's door closed and no one else remained in the gate area, I approached again to see about next steps. She looked at her schedule and said the next flight at 12:30 p.m. also looked full, and the 2:30 p.m. flight did not look any better. She smiled, but did not make me feel better, when she said, "Today does not look good for a student going to Denver."

I tried not to panic, but surely felt it. My enthusiasm for getting to Denver waned as I contemplated two, four, or six hours in the airport. *"Good grief, what if I cannot get out until tomorrow?"* ran through my mind.

After calling Hungie to let her know King was coming unaccompanied, I wandered up and down the concourse a bit biding my time. The anxiety built as the vagaries going with the student fare bore down on me. The uncertainty about King flying alone and me waiting for who knows how long, ate at me. I decided I needed something to occupy my mind, so I stopped at the next newsstand to peruse the offerings.

*Psycho-Cybernetics* was one on the best-seller shelf, offering positive wisdom and helpful insights on how to be a successful person. Only problem, I read it earlier in the year. One of its tenets dealt with worry over things you cannot control. The example given dealt with playing roulette and worrying after you placed your bet, and the wheel began spinning. At that point, the bettor can add nothing to his state of mind but anxiety, so the book says, relax and let the wheel spin out its result. I tried to apply it to the day I faced in the Seattle airport.

Another best seller was *Airport* by Arthur Hailey. The story dealt with everything that could go wrong at an airport during a huge snowstorm, and did. Not exactly the best reading to wait out an indeterminable stay at the airport, besides, I had read it too.

Passing up the best seller bookcase, I moved to the classics shelf and spied *Lady Chatterley's Lover*, by D. H. Lawrence. I only knew the U.S. authorities banned its unexpurgated edition for thirty years before an obscenity trial in the United Kingdom found it had literary merit. It appeared just the book to keep my mind off my situation.

Turns out it had fewer sensational sex descriptions than other things I had read, such as Terry Southern's *Candy*, which made the rounds in my dorm at South Plains College, but it did keep me busy for the day. Most people objected to its use of the f-word, but the book seemed to focus on the class differences between the lady and her workman more than a lascivious theme. Later, when telling others the tale of my day in the Seattle airport, I feigned sophistication by telling folks I read *Lady Chatterley's Lover*, while waiting for a plane.

I missed the 12:30, 2:30, and 4:30 p.m. flights to Denver and began to really worry. At each potential boarding my spirits rose only to fall once all the full-fare passengers arrived. One more chance for a 7 p.m. flight. After finishing my book and leaving it on a bench seat in Concourse C, I walked and walked trying to speed the waiting time. It did not work.

The 7 p.m. flight offered promise when the lady at the counter stamped my ticket and assigned a middle seat. Of course, she warned me my seat remained subject to bumping, if a full-fare passenger showed up at the last minute. They did not and I was on my way to Denver, fourteen hours after I arrived in Seattle. Alaska seemed a million miles away.

Hungie met my flight and informed me she and King had a good, but anxious day in Denver awaiting my arrival. She had picked him up from the United Baggage desk about mid-morning. After a quick dinner and a few tales of Alaska, I fell asleep as soon as my head hit the pillow.

## Back to School

A day of preparing for the rest of my journey followed while we made plans to travel to Morton and then Waco, Texas. On Monday morning we loaded two horses, the same Sweetness and Sugarfoot we had at Shoshoni, into a horse trailer hitched to Hungie's Pontiac GTO. Then we loaded all our gear into the trunk, added two dogs to the back seat, and a cat in a box carrier on the rear floorboard, and headed to Morton. The usual eight and a half to nine-hour drive took almost twelve, putting us into town after 8 p.m. The trip included two potty breaks for dogs and the cat, an exercise walking for the horses out of the trailer, and a twenty-minute brand inspection at the top of Raton Pass and the New Mexico border. The ride's entertainment consisted of me telling tales of Alaska, but I omitted any mention of the overly friendly neighbor.

Hungie headed to Waco with me because my daddy helped arrange a school teaching job for her. One of his Baylor classmates was the athletic director of the Waco public schools and did us a favor by securing a job in a junior high for her as a physical education teacher. She planned to teach while I finished my degree work at Baylor. I would keep my Resident Advisor job at Martin Hall until Thanksgiving, when we planned a wedding in St. Louis.

A Shoshoni alum finishing graduate work at Baylor helped us find a pasture to board the horses and we found a small rental house in south Waco for Hungie until I could join her. The dogs stayed at the house with her and the cat.

Hungie and I married at Thanksgiving in St. Louis as planned. I remained on track to graduate in May 1969, hoping to attend law school somewhere, Baylor, Colorado University, or Denver University. Of course, losing a student deferment by graduating left the specter of the Selective Service System lurking in the future, but I had a plan, which is another story.

The summer in Alaska remains a highlight in my life. Great adventure, the long drive and ferry ride to Alaska, exploring the state, seeing things never seen in Texas, catching a huge salmon on the Russian River, avoiding arrest by the Alaskan State Trooper after the fur and taxidermy debacle, and enjoying the summer with one of my best friends, all added to the mix of making a dream come true.

The following summers, 1969 and 1970, proved very different from the adventures in Alaska. Summers where I definitely did not control my destiny but had to react to cultural, societal, and governmental pressures to find my way. The tales of those events and how they shaped the person I became, come next.

# About the Author

Charles C. "Charlie" Ledbetter retired from a legal and consulting career spanning over forty years. As the Trail Boss for the Ledbetter Land & Cattle Company, Charlie is an accomplished public speaker, consultant to businesses, and author/publisher of nonfiction memoirs. He is the author of *Unexpected Conversations with Teenagers – A Spiritual Journey with Young Minds* and a series of books entitled *Look Out! Here Comes Summer – My*

*Incredible College Summers*. The series includes *A Teenager Goes to Washington – My Summer as a Congressional Intern – 1966*; *Shoshoni – My Summer as the Horse Wrangler – 1967*; and this book as the third book in the series when he traveled to Alaska for the summer with a longtime friend.

The series relates the author's adventures over the summers of his college years. He worked as a congressional intern in Washington, D.C.; a horse wrangler at an exclusive girls summer camp in Rollinsville, Colorado; and spent the summer in Alaska on the northern frontier. The final book in the series will cover graduating college, starting law school, receiving an induction notice for military service, and serving in the United States Marine Corps.

An avid reader and volunteer, he holds a B.A. in history from Baylor University and a Juris Doctor degree from the Sturm College of Law at the University of Denver. Charlie serves as the Historian for his local church.

Charlie is married, lives in Denver, Colorado near his two sons, enjoys attending varied activities of his four grandchildren, and is an avid photographer. He has traveled extensively, visiting five continents and twenty-six countries worldwide.

Readers may contact the author at charlescledbetter.com.

Made in the USA
Coppell, TX
29 May 2022

78259235R00141